D1759455

Mainstreaming Men into
Gender and Development:
Debates, Reflections, and Experiences

WITHDRAWN
FROM
UNIVERSITY OF PLYMOUTH
LIBRARY SERVICES

This book is to be returned on
or before the date stamped below

UNIVERSITY OF PLYMOUTH

PLYMOUTH LIBRARY

Tel: (01752) 232323
This book is subject to recall if required by another reader
Books may be renewed by phone
CHARGES WILL BE MADE FOR OVERDUE BOOKS

Oxfam

UNIVERSITY OF PLYMOUTH

Item No. 9005439979

Date − 1 APR 2003 Z−R

Class No. 305·31 CHA

Cont. No. ✓

PLYMOUTH LIBRARY

First published by Oxfam GB in 2000

© Oxfam GB 2000

ISBN 0 85598 451 1 ✓

A catalogue record for this publication is available from the British Library.

All rights reserved. Reproduction, copy, transmission, or translation of any part of this publication may be made only under the following conditions:

• With the prior written permission of the publisher; or
• With a licence from the Copyright Licensing Agency Ltd., 90 Tottenham Court Road, London W1P 9HE, UK, or from another national licensing agency; or
• For quotation in a review of the work; or
• Under the terms set out below.

This publication is copyright, but may be reproduced by any method without fee for teaching purposes, but not for resale. Formal permission is required for all such uses, but normally will be granted immediately. For copying in any other circumstances, or for re-use in other publications, or for translation or adaptation, prior written permission must be obtained from the publisher, and a fee may be payable.

Available from the following agents:

USA: Stylus Publishing LLC, PO Box 605, Herndon, VA 20172-0605, USA
tel: +1 (0)703 661 1581; fax: + 1(0)703 661 1547; email: styluspub@aol.com
Canada: Fernwood Books Ltd, PO Box 9409, Stn. 'A', Halifax, N.S. B3K 5S3, Canada
tel: +1 (0)902 422 3302; fax: +1 (0)902 422 3179; e-mail: fernwood@istar.ca
India: Maya Publishers Pvt Ltd, 113-B, Shapur Jat, New Delhi-110049, India
tel: +91 (0)11 649 4850; fax: +91 (0)11 649 1039; email: surit@del2.vsnl.net.in
K Krishnamurthy, 23 Thanikachalan Road, Madras 600017, India
tel: +91 (0)44 434 4519; fax: +91 (0)44 434 2009; email: ksm@md2.vsnl.net.in
South Africa, Zimbabwe, Botswana, Lesotho, Namibia, Swaziland: David Philip Publishers, PO Box 23408, Claremont 7735, South Africa
tel: +27 (0)21 674 4136; fax: +27(0)21 64 3358; email: dppsales@iafrica.com
Tanzania: Mkuki na Nyota Publishers, PO Box 4246, Dar es Salaam, Tanzania
tel/fax: +255 (0)51 180479, email: mkuki@ud.co.tz
Australia: Bush Books, PO Box 1958, Gosford, NSW 2250, Australia
tel: +61 (0)2 043 233 274; fax: +61 (0)2 092 122 468, email: bushbook@ozemail.com.au

Rest of the world: contact Oxfam Publishing, 274 Banbury Road, Oxford OX2 7DZ, UK.
tel. +44 (0)1865 311 311; fax +44 (0)1865 313 925; email publish@oxfam.org.uk

Printed by Oxfam Print Unit

Oxfam GB is a registered charity, no. 202 918, and is a member of Oxfam International.

Contents

Preface and acknowledgements

This report originated in research commissioned by the Latin America and Caribbean Division of the World Bank as part of a larger study being carried out by the Bank on men in gender and development. The project comprised a review of the small, but steadily growing, literature on men, masculinities, and development, and consultations with staff in nearly 30 development organisations in the UK and the USA. Oxfam, which has been at the forefront of enquiry and debate in men in gender and development, was a key participant in our survey. The present document adds to a pioneering body of work on the topic by Oxfam staff since the mid-1990s, and we are particularly grateful to Caroline Sweetman for her role in expediting publication.

Aside from the Bank-funded survey, the report draws from the first-hand field experience on men and masculinities of the two authors. Chant's work on this subject has been based in Costa Rica, with funding provided by the Nuffield Foundation (Award numbers: SOC/100[1554] and SGS/LB/0223) and the Economic and Social Research Council of the UK (Award number: R000222205). Gutmann's work in this field has been grounded primarily in Mexico, and has been financed over the years by grants from the following organisations: Brown University, Fulbright-Hays, National Institute of Mental Health, National Instititute on Alcohol Abuse and Alcoholism, National Science Foundation, University of California, and the Wenner-Gren Foundation.

Our work could not have been completed without the dedicated efforts of a small team comprising Carl McLean and Sam Goss (London School of Economics), and Hillary Crane (Brown University). These assistants conducted the bulk of the consultations with the staff and consultants attached to the development agencies in our survey. Using his background in gender theory, and own extensive field research on men and masculinities, Carl McLean also made a major contribution to designing our survey instrument. The project was received with considerable interest and co-operation among the individuals interviewed in the organisations, and we are immensely grateful to them for their time, ideas, and insights, all of which played a key role in shaping the report. Our gratitude also extends to colleagues who made suggestions for this project, many of whom read and commented on earlier versions of this document, namely Ramya Subrahmanian and Andrea Cornwall (Institute of Development Studies, Sussex); Javier Alatorre (Universidad Nacional Autónoma de México); Cathy McIlwaine (Queen Mary and Westfield College, University of London); Silvia Posocco (London School of Economics); José Olavarría (FLACSO, Santiago); Richard Parker (Columbia University and Instituto de Medicina Social, Universidade do Estado do Rio de Janeiro); Ruth Pearson (University of Leeds); Benno de Keijzer (Salud y Género, México); Caroline Moser (Overseas Development Institute, London); Juan Guillermo Figueroa (El Colegio de México) and Sangeetha Madhavan (Brown University). Special thanks are owed to Maria Correia of the World Bank for having asked us to conduct the study and arranged funding, and to Caren Levy, Development Planning Unit, University College London, for her kind assistance in conceptual orientation.

Despite the contributions of so many individuals and agencies, the findings, interpretations, and conclusions expressed in the paper are entirely those of the authors. They should not be attributed in any manner to Oxfam, or to the World Bank, its affiliated organisations, the members of its Board of Executive Directors, or the countries they represent.

Sylvia Chant
Matthew Gutmann
November 2000

List of abbreviations

CAFOD	Catholic Institute for International Development
CEC	Commission of the European Communities
CIDA	Canadian International Development Agency
CIIR	Catholic Institute for International Relations
DfID	Department for International Development
DPU	Development Planning Unit
FAO	Food and Agriculture Organisation
GAD	Gender and Development
GAM	Gender Analysis Matrix
GDI	Gender-related Development Index
GEM	Gender Empowerment Measure
HDI	Human Development Index
IADB	Inter-American Development Bank
ILO	International Labour Organisation
IMF	International Monetary Fund
IPPF	International Planned Parenthood Federation
MID	Men in Development
NGDO	Non-governmental Development Organisation
NGO	Non-governmental Organisation
ODI	Overseas Development Institute
PRA	Participatory Rural Appraisal
UN	United Nations
UNDP	United Nations Development Programme
UNESCO	United Nations Educational, Scientific, and Cultural Organisation
UNICEF	United Nations Children's Fund
UNIFEM	United Nations Development Fund for Women
USAID	United States Agency for International Development
VSO	Voluntary Service Overseas
WAD	Women and Development
WID	Women in Development

1 'Men-streaming' gender? Questioning new currents in gender and development policy

This paper provides a critical review of the desirability, potential, and prospects for a more male-inclusive approach to gender and development (GAD). Accepting that men have always been involved intentionally, indirectly, or otherwise, in a field concerned primarily with a vast range of inequities experienced by their female counterparts, the emphasis here is on men as gendered beings. The paper asks how their inclusion in gender and development analysis, policy, and practice might enhance work by and with women, to create a fairer deal for all involved in development interventions.

Our primary focus is on incorporating men in gender and development interventions at the grassroots. However, reflecting the importance attached to engaging men in moves to 'mainstream' gender (see below), there is also substantial discussion of male involvement in policy-making and planning on gender issues. The somewhat fanciful title we have given to this introductory chapter, and which sets the scene for the review as a whole, clearly plays on one of the most prevalent 'buzzwords' in the contemporary gender and development lexicon. It also provides a figurative analogy for the nature of our task. Streams may be fast- or slow-flowing, but always feed into greater bodies of water. They can also be managed or left to run their own course. The potential is there both to complement and compete with other occupants of the territory. By surveying the stream at an early stage, we arguably have chances to determine the most appropriate methods for ensuring that it sustains and enhances the broader terrain that is gender and development.

Why men? Why now?[1]

The reasons for our undertaking are many and varied, but one of the most significant is that the late twentieth century has seen 'men and masculinities' becoming an increasingly widely debated theme, not only in gender and development circles, but in the media, academia, politics, and popular culture. While the 1970s and 1980s were marked by an unprecedented focus on women among activists, scholars, practitioners, and policy-makers (not least on account of the UN Decade for Women), in the 1990s, a perceptibly larger share of the spotlight on gender has fallen on their male counterparts.

The question of 'why this rising interest in men and masculinities?' can in part be answered by the changes in gender relations in the world at large, especially in spheres such as employment, education, and family life. Although in the vast majority of countries women continue to bear a disproportionate share of material, social, and civil disadvantage, trends suggest that an increasing number of men, especially among the young and poor, are subject to mounting vulnerability and marginalisation. In various parts of the North and South, there is evidence that young men are beginning to fall behind their female counterparts in rates of educational attainment, and have less likelihood of obtaining employment (Chant and McIlwaine, 1998; Hearn, 1998; Kaztman, 1992). Declining prospects for assuming the economic responsibilities attached to the widely idealised male role of 'breadwinner' have undermined men's status and identities, and are often linked with their weakening integration into family units, especially as spouses and fathers (Escobar Latapí, 1998; Güendel and González, 1998; Moore, 1994; Silberschmidt, 1999; Williams, 1998). This, in turn, has been exacerbated by shifts in domestic power relations as women have entered the labour force in rising numbers and are increasingly heading their own households on a *de jure* or *de facto* basis (Chant, 1997a, 1999; Gutmann, 1996, 1998).[2] Rising emphasis in social policy on female household heads, and the intensification of social problems such as crime and violence, have been important corollaries of these trends (Sweetman, 1997:4; Moser and McIlwaine, 1999). In brief, we have moved into an era of widespread talk of 'men in crisis', 'troubled masculinities', and 'men at risk' (Chant, 2000a,b). Since many of the changes that feed these constructions have important implications for women, particularly those on low incomes, it is no surprise that curiosity and concern have stirred in various segments of the gender and development community.

Although men have long been present as a subject of gender and development analysis, (particularly in assessments of why gender and development initiatives so often fail), a more dedicated and overt interest in men and masculinities has emerged for other reasons. A major factor is a widely-shared aim of professionals in this field to disrupt the stubbornly persistent association of gender with women, and to carry through the spirit of 'gender mainstreaming' into practice. The 'mainstreaming' of gender concerns into development work is a relatively new and contested concept (as discussed in detail in Chapter 2). In broad terms, the objectives of 'mainstreaming' are to bring gender awareness from the sidelines to the centre of development planning, and to make gender issues an integral part of organisational thinking and practice. As defined by the Economic and Social Research Council of the United Nations:

Mainstreaming a gender perspective is the process of assessing the implications for women and men of any planned action, including legislation, policies or programmes in any area and at all levels. It is a strategy for making women's as well as men's concerns and experiences an integral dimension in the design, implementation, monitoring and evaluation of policies and programmes in all political, economic and societal spheres so that women and men benefit equally and inequality is not perpetuated. The ultimate goal is to achieve gender equality (cited in UNIFEM/CIDA-SEAGEP, 1998:6).

Calls for 'mainstreaming' have provoked attempts to develop new policies on the part of a wide range of government, non-government and multilateral institutions (Moser *et al.*, 1999:v). At the level of rhetoric, at least, the mid-1990s seems to have been something of a watershed regarding approaches to gender and development. As articulated by the UK's Department for International Development (DfID):

Before the 1995 World Conference on Women in Beijing, most efforts focused on addressing women's practical needs, and reducing the heavy burden placed on them by poverty and their multiple roles in the economy, the community and at home. After Beijing a more strategic approach has emerged which promotes full equality between women and men in all spheres of life, addressing the causes as well as the consequences of inequality and aiming to bring about fundamental changes in gender relations (DfID, 1998:1).

What this actually means in practice, however, seems somewhat indeterminate. Although discussions about men in gender and development are underway, there is scant evidence of 'male-inclusive' gender initiatives on the ground. Moreover, where these do exist, they tend to be restricted to a limited number of sectors such as sexual and reproductive health, and violence and conflict. These are areas in which the importance of gender relations is most direct and obvious, where the impacts of gender inequalities on women may be serious to the point of life-threatening, and where the need to engage men in transformational interventions is paramount. Even here, however, the issue of men is shrouded in uncertainty. In reproductive health, for example, the International Planned Parenthood Federation (1998:53) points out that:

There is no universally accepted understanding in this work of what it means to include men; rather a variety of interpretations exist of the concept of 'male involvement' and 'male responsibility'.

As for the broader sweep of development policy, there is scant evidence that a gender perspective (let alone a concern with women) has actually been central in any way, either at programme or planning levels. As MacDonald *et al.* (1997:8-9) assert:

There is today a rich and extensive body of documentation and literature dealing with women's subordinate position vis-à-vis men and the gendered nature and outcome of development processes ... Increased numbers of so-called mainstream development organisations have responded by formulating elaborate and detailed policy statements. Feminist discourse and insights have been incorporated into the policies of development bureaucracies such as the World Bank, United Nations agencies, national governments' overseas development ministries, international and national NG(D)Os and funding agencies. There is no doubt that gender is on the international agenda. But to what extent have institutions themselves really changed their practice? Are they accountable to the needs and aspirations of women?... Can historically male-dominated development agencies be transformed to the extent that goes beyond supporting the occasional women's project or appointing a gender expert?

Who is interested in men in gender and development?

In light of the above, it seems somewhat paradoxical that most current discussion about men in gender and development has occurred among women, rather than men.[3] Not only is it intriguing that men themselves are not clamouring for a say in these debates, but it is not as if women conceivably owe men a favour in this domain. Looking back at the 1970s, for example, one is hard-pressed to find evidence of men discussing how to 'get women into development', or lending active support to the feminist lobby.

This aside, and dismissing at the outset the idea that 'female altruism' may be held to account for the desire to 'bring men in from the cold', part of the reason for women's interest may have to do with the fact that the impetus for studies of masculinity has its roots in reflections on the condition of women, which is still a largely female domain (see Gomáriz, 1997:9). Another potentially important factor is that women continue to outnumber men in the field of gender and development, if not in development institutions more generally.

Although male development professionals are also involved in discussions of 'men and masculinity', for the most part these men are marginal to mainstream development planning, either by virtue of their membership of specific gender and development teams or units, or because of their lack of seniority in staff hierarchies (Pearson, 1999). The men who could arguably really make a difference to gender planning and mainstreaming, notably the directors and key decision-makers in multilateral and bilateral donor agencies, are conspicuous by their absence. What is also clear, is that whereas the 'women in development' (WID) campaigns of the 1970s were grounded in Second Wave feminist anti-imperialist politics, there is no parallel political movement pushing for the incorporation of men in gender and develop-ment. The interest in men and masculinities can accordingly be seen has having arisen out of a development brief, rather than any discernible political impetus (ibid.).

Women's views on men in gender and development

Aside from the suggestion that women's majority presence in gender and development analysis and planning has rendered them the prime movers in discussions of men and masculinity, it is important to ask if there are reasons why women might be particularly interested in bringing men into gender and development. Although there is no identifiable body of enquiry or literature on this subject to date, it is possible to detect a number of diverse positions on the issue of 'engaging men'.

At one end of the spectrum, the idea of including men might be explained by a concern to 'redress the balance' in a field that has traditionally been heavily dominated by women. In some senses this mirrors the arguments of the 1970s for including women in development (Pearson, 1999). While women 'being fair to men' is plausibly driven by a sense of justice, or by the idea that setting 'good examples' of gender equality and equity might meet with reciprocal concessions, a potentially critical factor is the broader move in development policy from a 'needs-' to a 'rights-based' approach. To deny men's rights is to deny the universality of human rights which, although a contested and contentious arena, has become a major vehicle for legitimising women's struggles, especially with regard to reproductive health (see Hardon and Hayes [eds], 1997; MacDonald, 1995; Tomasevski, 1994)

Leading on from this, it seems likely that some of the impetus to broaden out the scope of gender interventions derives from recognition of the fact that men as well as women may be constrained and disadvantaged by gender divisions and disparities. As Sweetman (1998), among others, points out, women are not the only losers. As indicated earlier, this is something that has come into particularly sharp relief in the late twentieth and early twenty-first centuries. Bringing men under closer scrutiny could help to disrupt the common dichotomy in gender analysis between the 'tender attention to female subjectivities and the analytically crude cardboard cut-outs of pampered sons and patriarchs' (Jackson, 1999). This may lead to fuller acknowledgement of the ways in which rigid gender systems prejudice men as well as women. In turn, the potential arises to broaden and strengthen vested interests in changing the status quo.

Related in many ways to the above is the fact that interest in men may be the product of a shift towards a focus on 'gender relations' (rather than women) in gender and development analysis and policy. Indeed, male exclusion is untenable if the conceptual underpinnings of contemporary rhetoric about gender and development are to be realised in practice (Chant, 2000a). Moreover, given widespread observations that the gender and development movement has probably gone as far as it can in terms of making the case for women, a readiness to talk about men with a view to their greater incorporation signals both maturity and healthy evolution. Added to this is the growing recognition of the multiple and fragmented nature of people's identities whereby, in certain situations, it becomes entirely possible to conceive of mutualities in men's and women's interests and strategic alliances for change. In this way, 'planning for the other half' (White, 1994) could add up to a much more fruitful whole.

Towards the other end of the spectrum, it might be conjectured that interest in men and masculinities is being advanced *by* women, *for* women, in their own interests. In other words, the move to bring men into gender and development is spearheaded by women because they think they have something to gain. It is now widely recognised, for example, that women-only approaches to development have very limited impacts on gender relations. In this light, involving men may be seen as a more effective alternative for scaling down gender inequalities. Whether or not this particular position on men goes beyond an instrumentalist 'technical fix' to encompass broader political considerations, however, remains unclear.

Last but not least, it is important to bear in mind that not all women are deeply interested in 'men and masculinities' in gender and development, and some are hostile. For some women, the current interest in men and masculinities is nothing more than a passing fad; for others it represents an unjustifiable detraction from the struggle to make women's concerns as central as men's in development policy. A large number of women are also suspicious about the possible end product of a process which may open doors to men without due consideration of the potential consequences. Just as reframing 'women's issues' as 'gender issues' has often provided an excuse for development institutions to do nothing, giving men a bigger place in gender policy could make matters worse. Questions of power and privilege are crucial here and should not be glossed over. As MacDonald *et al.* (1997:11) remind us:

Since gender refers to both women and men, it has been easy to misconstrue gender as a neutral concept, obscuring or denying the fact that, in the world as it is at present, gender relations are a hierarchy with men at the top.

Notwithstanding the possibility that some men, as well as women, may gain from changes in gender relations (see Metcalf and Gomez, 1998;

White, 1994), is it really possible to engage men in a process that is likely to deprive them of entitlements, and to demean their authority along the way? Can men truly share power with women? What are the implications of men having rights as well as responsibilities in gender and development? What tactics are necessary to ensure that male inclusion does not ride roughshod over the concerns of women? To what extent is an 'add men and stir' approach (the equivalent of which failed decisively for their female counterparts back in the 1970s) a more appropriate strategy than transforming gender and development approaches in their entirety?

At the bottom line, such questions are born out of very real fears that making way for men may eclipse women's primacy in a field which they themselves staked out against major odds and which has been marked by struggle ever since. 'Letting men in' (in anything other than a secondary capacity at least), could be regarded as 'letting go' of a terrain in which women have won a legitimate claim to their own, albeit limited, resources. This issue is redolent with material, social, and political dimensions — both for women in development organisations and their counterparts at the grassroots — and is possibly the biggest sticking point when it comes to including issues of masculinity in gender and development.

Despite the tentative, and somewhat chaotic, state of questioning on men and masculinities in gender and development, it is apparent that there are already numerous tensions sur-rounding male inclusion in policy and practice. No-one seems to be clear as to where current discussions might lead, and the chances are that these will become considerably more heated down the line. Given, however, that women have led these debates, that women-only development strategies have been limited in their impacts, and that men's lives and identities are currently caught in a groundswell of transition, it is arguably an opportune moment during which to reflect on whether enquiry and concern with men might be harnessed in such as a way as to enhance strategies and outcomes in the future.

It should be emphasised at the outset, however, that *reflection*, rather than advocacy, is the guiding spirit of this document. Moreover, given the relative novelty of the subject matter, our concern is primarily with contextualising the evolution of interest in men, and with raising issues, rather than proposing solutions or guidelines. Since the question of male inclusion in gender and development is likely to be anything but straightforward, and will most certainly be long drawn-out, we conceive this study as a modest starting point, which, as far as possible, attempts to explore the often dissonant views of different stakeholders.

There being even less consensus on men in gender and development than women in the same, our liberal use of citations and pointers to references is an attempt to do justice to the many voices and opinions to be found in this new and exciting domain, as well as an effort to overcome the fact that the consultative part of our exercise has been restricted to the North. We also stress that we do not wish to raise false hopes. We do not want to give the impression that gender and development policy — with or without men — can do much to change the world, or that, regardless of all the efforts people have made in this area, there are real choices for development professionals, let alone women (and men) on the ground. By the same token, one small, but arguably significant, fact is that this project itself involved both women and men, working in a team in which co-operation and consensus have reigned persistently over conflict. Given the potentially controversial and divisive nature of the subject matter, this experience gives a modest indication that collaboration in the interests of subverting the systematic reproduction of inequality might well be the best way forward.

Structure of the report

The report contains six chapters. This first one has identified the rationale for the study and flagged-up some of the key issues and potential controversies surrounding 'men and masculinities' in gender and development. The following chapter cements the context of the investigation by reviewing the evolution of WID/GAD policy approaches and gender analysis frameworks, and exploring the extent to which these have made space for men. In light of the relatively minor in-roads made thus far, Chapter 3 proceeds to identify why gender and development approaches remain overwhelmingly oriented towards women.

Chapter 4 is a preponderantly speculative chapter. It considers principles and rationales for including men in the conceptualisation, operationalisation, and implementation of gender and development policies. Although largely hypothetical, the review draws attention to some of the key problems that have arisen from 'male exclusion', as well as to the potential gains to be derived from men's inclusion.

The focus of Chapter 5 is how far the issue of 'men in development' has been a feature in the actual gender and development practices of development organisations to date. Drawing on consultations with approximately 30 multi-laterals, national development institutions, and non-government organisations (NGOs) in the UK and USA, the chapter aims to review current 'in-house' approaches to gender and development, and to explore the extent to which men are actively engaged at policy-making, operational, and grassroots levels. A key focus of the discussion is the kinds of impacts that experiences of male inclusion have had on the procedural context, design, implementation, and outcomes of GAD policies.

Moving beyond some of the 'whys' and 'wherefores', the main focus of Chapter 6 is *tactics*. In which ways might gender and development policy realistically move towards a more gender-balanced, male-inclusive approach?

Appendix 1 consists of the details of the survey instrument on men and gender and development policy used in consultation with development agencies. Appendix 2 lists the individuals and organisations consulted.

2 Men: a missing factor in gender and development policy?

Introduction

It is widely recognised that the concepts of 'gender and development' and 'women and development' have frequently been construed as one and the same thing, and often not mistakenly. Although the last three decades have seen an increasing range of analytical and policy approaches to gender and development, their origins in concern with women's disadvantage (and for the most part in feminist politics) have proved extremely persistent. While a general move in umbrella policy approaches from 'Women in Development' (WID) to 'Gender and Development' (GAD) has embodied greater reference to men, and arguably created greater space for the inclusion of men as actors and clients in gender interventions, strong and substantive recommendations to 'bring men on board' remain rare thus far.

With this in mind, the aims of the present chapter are to explore the evolution of approaches to gender analysis and policy, to identify where men are situated in these approaches, and to examine in which ways, and for what reasons, men's importance as a constituency has started to grow.

Policy approaches to gender and development: from WID to GAD

Although there has long been considerable diversity in approaches to gender and development, their conceptual underpinnings can be broadly discerned as having shifted from a WID to GAD orientation over time. Although these orientations are in themselves diverse, in crude terms WID tends to focus on women as a group in their own right, whereas GAD gives precedence to gender relations.

Although WID and GAD are often presented as dichotomous approaches (see for example, Moser, 1993:3-4), the fact that GAD evolved out of WID is extremely important, both in terms of contemporary manifestations of GAD (particularly in a practical and applied sense), and in

respect of men's hitherto marginal (and oppositional) role in the field of gender and development. As such, brief backgrounds and characterisations of these policy approaches are helpful in pinpointing the state of men's incorporation into the design and implementation of gender and development initiatives.

Background to WID

The formulation of the term 'WID' dates to the early 1970s, and is commonly attributed to the Women's Committee of the Washington DC Chapter of the Society for International Development. Concern with women's 'predicament' in developing regions was fuelled by a mounting body of academic research, revealing that 'gender-blindness' in the design and execution of development projects resulted in women being 'overlooked', sidelined, and even harmed, by such interventions (Moser, 1993:2). The term crossed swiftly into the policy arena with its incorporation into the 'WID approach' by the United States Agency for International Development (USAID) (ibid.). Based on the notion that women represented an 'untapped' force in economic growth, and galvanised by accelerating claims around the world for a fairer deal for women in development, the WID movement entered its heyday during the UN Decade for Women (1975-1985). The call to 'integrate' women in development provoked the formation of 'national machineries' to fulfil this objective in around 140 countries (del Rosario, 1997:77; see also Alvarez, 1998:302). This was complemented by larger-scale initiatives such as the establishment of women's representatives, bureaux/units, and programmes in regional and international organisations including the Canadian International Development Agency, the European Union, the World Bank, the United Nations and the International Labour Organization. These developments were parallelled in numerous NGOs such as Oxfam, Christian Aid, and Voluntary Service Overseas (VSO) (see CEC, 1992; Jahan, 1995:62-4; Lotherington and Flemmen, 1991; Pietilä and Vickers, 1994; UNDP, 1995; Versteylen, 1994).

Table 2.1: Main WID policy approaches

Approach	Target group	Time period	Brief characterisation
Equity approach	Women	1975–85	First WID approach. Main goal is to accomplish women's equality with men in development, through changing legal and institutional frameworks that subordinate women.
Anti-poverty approach	Low-income women/ Female heads of household	1970s onwards	Second WID approach. Premised on the idea that women's disadvantage stems from poverty, rather than gender subordination, the main aim is to raise women's economic status through income-generating programmes.
Efficiency approach	Low-income women	1980s onwards	Third WID approach. Main goal is to harness women's efforts to make development more efficient and to alleviate poverty in the wake of neo-liberal economic restructuring.

Sources: Levy (1999); Moser (1993); Moser *et al.* (1999)

WID contributions and critiques

While different types of WID policy emerged during the 1970s and 1980s (see Table 2.1 for summary), three common factors stand out: a focus on women as an 'analytical and operational category', the setting-up of separate organisational structures for dealing with women, and the development of women-specific policies and projects (Levy, 1996:1 *et seq.*). At one level, these contributions signalled a major breakthrough for women: never before had resources been apportioned to women's development in this way, nor had so many women infiltrated the ranks of the international development system. This potential for injecting awareness of gender inequality into development planning was a first.

At another level, however, the shared tendency of WID approaches to concentrate exclusively on women provoked increasingly widespread doubts about their efficacy and desirability. In conceptual terms, for example, the essentialising notion of women as a group whose condition was primarily determined by their sex, sat uneasily with rising theoretical emphasis on the need to understand how women's positions evolved dynamically through their socially-constructed relationships with men. Leading out of this, concerns emerged around WID's seemingly unquestioned assumption that women would benefit by being 'slotted in' to existing (male-biased) development structures (Parpart, 1995:227). This presupposed that women's development was a 'logistical problem, rather than something requiring a fundamental reassessment of gender relations and ideology' (Parpart and Marchand, 1995:13). Another major problem was WID's failure to broach the social differentiation of women on account of age, class, ethnicity, and so on (Moser, 1993:3; Pearson and Jackson, 1998:3). The definition of 'women in general' as a single identifiable interest group could obviously obscure the effects of other 'cross-cutting differences', which might be equally, if not more, important than gender *per se* in respect of understanding and addressing inequality (Cornwall, 1998:50). As summed up by Kabeer and Subrahmanian (1996:8):

The absurdity of the assumption that programmes can be devised for some category called women becomes clear when it is considered how far planners would attempt to devise a project for some undifferentiated category called men. Questions would immediately be asked about 'which men?'.

The fact of the matter is that within gender and development (as opposed to development more generally), these questions have rarely been asked. This, in turn, is arguably a major factor in WID's seemingly limited impact on reducing gender inequalities. Sara Longwe (1995:18), among others, for example, questions the relevance of WID efforts when the last two decades have witnessed if not a deterioration, than at least a stagnation, of women's positions in so many developing countries. Although the process of measuring and interpreting change in people's lives is fraught with difficulty, one widely observed tendency is the so-called 'feminisation of poverty' (see also Williams, 1999:179).[1] Described as a 'tragic consequence of women's unequal access to economic opportunities' (UNDP, 1995:36), more than 70 per cent of the world's 1.3 billion people in poverty are female, and the situation is getting worse. The increased likelihood of poverty having 'a woman's face' (ibid.) is hard to explain given that:

... after the 1985 World Conference on Women, all major development agencies altered their policies to ensure a better focus on various aspects of women's equality and empowerment. We are left with the question why such a large collective development policy has produced virtually no results (Longwe, 1995:18).

Part of the problem with WID was that while it forced a necessary visibility of women in the development process, its tendency to generate *ad hoc* or 'add-on' solutions conspired to produce 'tokenism and marginalisation of women's long-term interests' (MacDonald *et al.*, 1997:11). This resonates not only on the ground, but at all levels of the planning process,

with Levy (1998:259) noting that: 'Separate policies on women or gender on their own have been shown to be unsuccessful in directing gender integration into mainstream policy.'

Related to this, a rising tide of resistance from women in the South against the imposition of neo-colonial development strategies generated major doubt over whether women would benefit by being drawn further into a process of planned change that not only prioritised external interests, but had routinely been responsible for widening gender disparities and causing adverse outcomes in women's lives (see Sen and Grown, 1988). Even with 'gender-aware' (as opposed to 'gender-blind') programmes, the advantages to women were often heavily circumscribed by WID's orientation to treating the symptoms, rather than the sources, of gender inequalities. These concerns led, at one level, to the emergence of calls for development grounded within the self-determined interests of Southern women (encapsulated broadly in what has come to be known as the 'Empowerment approach').[2] At a more general level, criticisms of WID transformed themselves steadily into building blocks for a new 'GAD' paradigm (see Table 2.2).

Table 2.2: Main policy approaches post-WID and GAD

Approach	Target group	Time period	Brief characterisation
Empowerment	Women	1980s onwards	First post-WID approach, sometimes referred to as 'WAD' ('Women and Development'). Aims to empower women and to strengthen their self-reliance by means of supporting bottom-up/grassroots mobilisation.
Integration	Women and men	1980s onwards	First GAD approach. Concern is to counteract the marginalisation of WID by integrating gender as a cross-cutting issue in development organisations and interventions (often referred to as 'mainstreaming').
Equality	Women and men	1990s	Second GAD approach, emerging in the aftermath of the Fourth World Conference for Women at Beijing. Goal is to achieve equality and power-sharing between men and women as means, and end, of wider exercise of human rights, and people-centred sustainable development.

Sources: Levy (1999); Moser (1999)

Note: Levy (1999) also identifies the emergence in the 1990s of GAD versions of Equity, Efficiency, and Anti-Poverty approaches which, in contrast with their WID predecessors, nominally consider men as well as women.

The emergence of GAD

With the core of the Empowerment approach lying in 'feminist theorising and action grounded in Southern realities' (Parpart and Marchand, 1995:14), women's subordination is viewed as rooted both in neo-colonial oppression and in gender relations (Andersen, 1992:175). Despite its overt concern with women, therefore, the Empowerment approach's recognition of the multi-relational contingency of gender makes it more closely aligned with GAD than WID thinking. In turn, and particularly in respect of its emphasis on participatory development and its desire to transform power relations at all levels of development planning, GAD draws considerable amounts of inspiration from the Empowerment paradigm.

GAD in theory

Although GAD has been interpreted in different ways by different stakeholders,[3] its basic theoretical premise is that gender identity is a dynamic social construct. Not only is it shaped by a multiplicity of interacting time- and place-contingent influences (culture, mode of production, legal and political institutions, for example), but it is further mediated by men's and women's insertion into other socially-generated categories such as class, age, and 'race' (Moser, 1993:3). In this light, an undifferentiated and unilateral focus on women is not only concep-tually inappropriate, but deprives gender inter-ventions of their transformative potential. Only by accepting that gender identity is a constructed rather than a 'natural' part of life does radical change in gender roles and relations become possible (Parpart and Marchand, 1995:14). In turn, planning for change in women's lives clearly entails changes for men, with structural shifts in male–female power relations being 'a necessary precondition for any development process with long-term sustainability' (Rathgeber, 1995:212). Following on from this, while the short-term goals of GAD are often decidedly similar in character to those of WID (for example, improved education, access to credit, and legal rights for women), these are nominally conceived as stepping stones towards long-term goals encompassing 'ways to empower women through collective action, to encourage women to challenge gender ideologies and institutions that subordinate women' (Parpart, 1995:235-6).

The priority accorded to women's needs and interests in GAD is justified by the fact that because 'gender relations almost universally favour men and disadvantage women, explicit and on-going recognition of women's subordinate position in the gender hierarchy is necessary' (MacDonald *et al.*, 1997:11). The responsibility for change, however, lies with men and women at all levels of the development process (Kanji,1995:2). The issue of *responsibility* is an all-important factor in the quest for gender equity, as illustrated by an evaluation of a gender training programme for male community organisers in the Indian state of Tamil Nadu, facilitated by men from Canada and Nicaragua:

If women hold up half the sky, then they cannot hold up more than their half of the responsibilities towards gender change. Organisers and participants alike agreed that men of conscience should play more than just a supportive role in this search for justice. Given the critical leadership positions of many men in social movements, to expect anything less would be self-defeating (Goodwin, 1997:6).

GAD approaches call for 'gender relations' (rather than women) to be adopted as the primary analytical tenet, and for the integration of a gender perspective in all development activities, and at all levels of the development planning process (Levy, 1996:2). The term 'gender perspective' is crucially important, meaning a form of seeing, thinking about, and doing development, thereby moving away from the frequently bland efforts implied by labels such as 'gender component' or 'gender dimension'. Strong statements reflecting this conceptual (and political) shift from what Kabeer and Subrahmanian (1996:1) call 'attempts to *integrate* gender into pre-existing policy concerns and attempts to *transform* mainstream policy agendas from a gender perspective' are increasingly found in the documentation of national development agencies. Working within a framework of sustain-able development, for example, the Norwegian government declares its intention to promote:

... equal rights and opportunities for women and men in all areas of society. It is not enough for development assistance to apply to individual projects directed towards women. Equal rights and opportunities for women and men must be integrated into all aspects of development cooperation. It is not a question of simply changing the attitudes and behaviour of individual women and men. If the process of creating equal rights for women and men is to succeed, a radical development process at a national level is required. This in turn requires political will. It is a question of long-term change stemming from society's need to utilise the knowledge and experience of both women and men (Royal Ministry of Foreign Affairs, 1997:1).[4]

Emphatically not to be confused with the integration of gender into conventional 'mainstream' (male-determined, male-biased) development, 'GAD mainstreaming' is about re-working structures of decision-making and institutional cultures so that gender is dealt with centrally, sustainably, and organically, as opposed to peripherally, sporadically, and mechanically. As MacDonald *et al.* (1997:12) suggest:

The gender dimension cannot be 'added' to an agency's values or practice; it is already there, because all aspects of an agency's functioning are affected by gender relations within the agency and in its relations with its interlocutors.

Indeed, with the shift from WID to GAD, which arguably has brought sharper realisation of the entrenchment of gender inequalities in development organisations themselves (March *et al.*, 1999:9), 'in-house' issues, such as staffing and promotion, access to parental leave and support, inter-personal relations between colleagues, and so on, come into the remit, alongside the promotion of gender-aware attitudes and approaches to development planning (Kajifusa, 1998:4).

At the level of policy-making and operations, evolving GAD orthodoxy contends that although it may remain useful, not to mention essential, to maintain specialist gender units within institutions, these should be accompanied by the 'creation of gender competence among staff of existing structures' (Levy, 1996:2). This can be facilitated by training, accountability measures for good gender practices, building gender networks in organisations, and so on, such that responsibilities for ensuring gender equity are diffused throughout organisations (see ActionAid, 1998:11). In turn, all programmes should entail a gender perspective, with targeted female- and male-specific initiatives being accompanied by the factoring-in of gender into mainstream sector-specific interventions (ibid.). At its logical extreme, this approach carries the potential of placing gender-awareness and fairness at the very heart of development planning, with far-reaching implications for the everyday lives of practitioners and beneficiaries (Commonwealth Secretariat, 1995a:14).

GAD dilemmas and debates

However, despite the fact that 'mainstreaming gender' has much initial appeal, it is critical to bear in mind that GAD has only recently begun to be adopted by institutions, and that the number of evaluations undertaken of GAD to date are too few to allow for a proper evaluation of its impact on development policy and practice (Levy, 1996:2). In turn, there is quite widespread agreement that while the principles of GAD may be positive and persuasive, the question of how best to translate these into practice requires considerably more attention. As Humble (1998:36), among others, has asserted: 'GAD still remains a theory in need of a methodology for implementation'.

Within the space waiting to be filled by 'best practice' recommendations, a major debate has emerged around the most appropriate tactics for organising the integration of gender in institutions. Are GAD-specific machineries still necessary in organisations, or do they perpetuate the traditional isolation of women's and gender concerns from mainstream programming? As Porter, Smyth, and Sweetman (1999:8) observe in relation to their experience of Oxfam GB's specialist gender unit at headquarters: '... a specialist unit can become a ghetto, where individuals are isolated and their work marginalised'. Moreover, even though Oxfam's specialist gender unit has now been replaced by a multi-disciplinary team as part of the 'mainstreaming' process, it still seems difficult for its members to make gender issues matter in the way they would like. Suzanne Williams (1999:185), a member of Oxfam since 1977, founder of Oxfam's specialist gender unit in 1985 (then called the Gender and Development Unit — GADU), and currently Gender and Human Rights Adviser in the Oxfam Policy Department, writes:

... from my position now, and remembering the beginnings of GADU, I see that the same challenges and problems remain. Gender work is still catalytic and advisory; peripheral not core ... we still find ourselves in the sidestream, battling to get gender into the mainstream, rather than determining the course of the stream itself.

For the above reasons, some have argued that the women's agenda needs to be much more forcefully addressed, such that '... instead of trying to fit gender issues into every sector, the focus should move towards an agenda-setting approach' (Jahan, 1995:126). Indeed, in the absence of such a strategy, the dispersal of responsibilities for GAD may not achieve the stated aim of producing a more prominent positioning of gender, but instead obliterate or subvert struggles that women have fought long and hard to win.

Another important issue within this debate is whether making gender issues part of the institutional routine depoliticises and/or dilutes the feminist content of gender initiatives. Theoretically, this should not occur, given that changes in organisational administration can be part of a larger political strategy to transform structures of power (ActionAid, 1998:4). In practice, however, there is evidence that feminist ideas have backed into the 'closet' as a means of winning approval and resources for gender initiatives in development organisations (see Smyth, 1999). On balance, however, it would seem inadvisable to eliminate GAD-specific machinery, until there is more convincing evidence for fundamental changes in gender attitudes and relations in organisations. In the light of the importance of hedging bets at this relatively early stage of GAD history, it is no surprise that a 'twin-track approach' has tended to be regarded as the most appropriate option:

The current consensus seems to be that organisations need to use both approaches — integrating gender concerns throughout the organisation, as well as maintaining specialist departments or units — in order to avoid marginalisation and co-optation of gender issues (March *et al.*, 1999:10).

Connected with the preceding point, rather longer-established debates continue regarding head-counts of male and female staff in development agencies. Some see numbers of women and men as relatively unimportant in advancing gender concerns in the work of the organisation, so long as people are gender-trained, gender-aware, and gender-accountable. Yet in the light of the common observation that, even if gender training is used, it will go to waste where men and women lack the support of a clear gendered policy framework and/or gender-aware procedures (Levy, 1998:261), many feel that building a critical female mass inside development organisations should remain paramount (Karl, 1995:103). This is exemplified in a forceful, though contentious, statement by the head of UNIFEM-Bangkok, Lorraine Corner (1998:72):

When qualified and experienced women comprise approximately half of the planners, bureaucrats and politicians, the objectives of mainstreaming will have been achieved and the gender dimension will automatically become an integral part of policy-making and planning.

Another potential problem in need of more attention in GAD debates revolves around how we conceptualise gender relations, and what kinds of gender relations might be determined as making a real difference to women and men. As Cornwall (1998:52) notes, all too frequently 'gender relations' are used as a 'shorthand for relationships that are regarded as inherently oppositional and that describe particular relations between women and men' (usually those between sexual partners). A more differentiated understanding of gender relations, which embraces the variety and complexity of relations between different groups of women and men, including those that are potentially co-operative as well as conflictive, would appear vital in order to transport GAD beyond the bounds of theoretical supposition. Under this heading, it is also useful to think about the eligibility of different male stakeholders. In the draft gender policy of Womankind Worldwide, a UK charity, for example, it is stated that the organisation will work directly with men who support women's emancipation, and who eschew violence against women and girls (Johnstone, 1999:7). Yet it is uncertain whether these men need training first, and exactly how they might benefit from training if they already have the 'right attitudes'.

Leading on from the above, and in respect of the principal concerns of the present document, one of the most pressing issues for GAD is that of the place and participation of men in gender and development policy and planning. Doubts and uncertainties abound in this regard, and although men are clearly present as a conceptual entity, practically their presence is all but invisible. This is possibly because of the lack of a clear vision and agenda, born out of uncertainty about where men are coming from in the gender struggle, and how they can actually be engaged to move it forward:

... feminist scholars have seldom argued about how men can be committed to gender issues. This appears to be a significant contradiction which assumes that women and men can challenge gender inequality against women on an equal footing, whereas it is too often mentioned that a majority of men are resistant and few men are supportive. How can men and women share an ends and means for the transformation? The argument of gender mainstreaming alone is insufficient unless one makes men an issue (Kajifusa, 1998:7).

Although the conceptual basis of GAD renders men's involvement central to the success of GAD strategies, there are few guidelines on how to ensure such involvement. On the one hand, this is not surprising, given lack of experience of involving men in 'gender programmes' at any level, the primary concern of GAD with women's disadvantage, and the problems of navigating a path likely to be strewn with numerous obstacles and conflicts. Given that '... the transformation of gender relations has to be a transformatory *political process*' (ActionAid, 1998:4, emphasis in original), not only are there questions of power and politics to be negotiated at every turn, but it could also be levelled that gender relations — which, by definition, are multivariant and dynamic — are a 'slippery' entity in development planning, and extremely difficult to deal with pragmatically. Instead of an identifiable target group, the main concern becomes the space between two (internally differentiated) sets of actors. Working with the concept of gender relations demands that substantive tactical issues be broached. Failure to do so has potentially far-reaching implications. First, reference to men may be no more than an act of 'window-dressing', much in the way that rhetoric about, and interventions for, women have often been a smokescreen for 'non-action' as far as confronting fundamental gender inequalities is concerned. Second, when the practicalities of including men are ill-defined, development agency personnel may be understandably unwilling to take risks, and fall back on the old WID-centred approach instead. It could prove impossible ever to identify the extent to which a gender-relations approach is actually the most appropriate method for achieving equality between men and women in the context of development assistance.

Notwithstanding the importance of making more solid progress in the trying and testing of male-inclusive gender initiatives at the grassroots, some 'productive speculation', and observations from experience, have appeared in some segments of the development planning literature.

One idea revolves around the importance of *flexibility*, with Caren Levy (1999) noting that, depending on the orientation of the project in question, strategic choices may have to be made about whether to focus on women, on men, or on women and men conjointly (see also MacDonald *et al.*, 1997:11). Phasing is likely to be highly relevant here, especially given the need for long-term, rather than one-off, interventions in gender relations, and the tendency for change in this arena to take place 'one step at a time' (Goodwin, 1997:6).

Another contribution is the suggestion to provide means for *conflict resolution*. In her work on participatory rural appraisal (PRA) and GAD, for example, Morag Humble (1998) observes the fundamental tension between the need for men to be involved in gender projects, but at the same time, the importance of allowing women to define their own needs, goals, and strategies. In order to reconcile these contradictions, she argues that 'mechanisms for managing and diffusing conflict' are likely to be an essential requirement of GAD methodology (Humble, 1998: 37).

A third suggestion is that *male development workers* should be brought into the process of gender work as a means of gaining acceptance from male target groups, and for helping to dispense with the idea that gender is only about women (Cornwall, 1998:54; Tadele, 1999).

Fourth and finally, *tact and sensitivity* are likely to be a *sine qua non* for nurturing men's allegiance to gender. This may involve (female) development workers taking a sympathetic and non-trivialising stance towards the sacrifices men may have to make to break with certain gender roles (Bhasin, 1997:61). Strategic routes to defuse men's potential resistance to gender may also entail trying to raise gender issues at the grassroots in a 'non-threatening' way, possibly by reframing 'women's issues' in terms of power rather than gender relations *per se* (Cornwall, 1998:54).

Reinforcing the third point, the use of men to facilitate gender training workshops with men has also proved to be helpful in experiences of using the Gender Analysis Matrix, a participatory planning tool that forms part of a growing range of gender analysis frameworks, identified briefly below.

Gender analysis frameworks

The bases of different gender policy approaches lie not only in different political and social goals, but also draw from, as well as shape, the methodologies used to explore gender at the grassroots. While these frameworks are discussed comprehensively elsewhere (March *et al.*, 1999), it is interesting to note that out of the eight main models currently used by practitioners (see Table 2.3), men figure prominently in only two of them. This is not to say, however, that the others necessarily exclude men, and the mere fact that most involve gathering baseline data on men provides an important foundation. As March *et al.* (1999:26) observe:

In practice, gender-analysis frameworks do not tend to be used to plan interventions which target men or boys. However, a gender analysis should take place for all interventions because they have a potential impact on gender relations, and therefore on both sexes.

12

Table 2.3: Gender analysis frameworks

Framework	Brief summary
Harvard Framework	One of the first gender analysis frameworks. Uses 'grid' or 'matrix' to organise collection of gender-disaggregated data at household and community level. This comprises four main components: activity profile, access and control profile, factors influencing constraints and opportunities, and checklist for project-cycle analysis. Main aim is to make an economic case for allocating resources to women.
People-oriented Planning Framework	Offshoot of Harvard Framework, adapted for use in refugee situations. Collects and organises gender-disaggregated data in activities and use and control of resources, with reference to political context and with emphasis on change and participation. Main aim is to stimulate more efficient use and more appropriate targeting of development assistance for displaced populations.
Moser Framework	Encompasses three main concepts: women's triple role; practical and strategic gender needs (Box 2.1); and categories of WID/GAD policy approaches. Explores gender roles, control of resources and decision-making within households, practical and strategic gender needs, and aims of different types of policy intervention, with a view to planning for the balancing of women's triple role. Main aim is women's emancipation from their subordination.
Gender Analysis Matrix (GAM)	'Bottom-up' participatory planning tool which emphasises the fundamental importance of people's own analysis of gender in the promotion of transformation. Uses matrix for the generation of information on four main areas: labour, time, resources, and socio-cultural factors, at four levels of society: women, men, households, and community. Main aim is to facilitate community's own diagnosis and strategies for self-directed change.
Capacities and Vulnerabilities Framework	Designed for use in humanitarian and disaster relief-and-preparedness interventions. Framework premised on notion that people's existing 'capacities' and 'weaknesses' (e.g. physical/material, social organisational, cultural, and psychological) condition the impacts of, and responses to, crisis. Disaggregates communities not only by gender but by other social relations such as age and socio-economic status. Main aim is to assist in meeting people's immediate needs in crises, and to achieve sustainable social and economic development in the longer term.
Women's Empowerment (Longwe) Framework	An approach that explores the extent to which women's concerns are recognised in development initiatives, and which addresses the progression of women's equality and empowerment through five basic levels: welfare, access, conscientisation, participation, and control. Main aim is to assist planners to problematise what women's empowerment and equality mean in practice.
Social Relations (Kabeer) Framework	An approach which scrutinises the dynamic and interacting structural relationships which create and perpetuate social divisions in four main institutional spaces: the household, community, the market, and the state. Main aim is to assist in the analysis of gender inequalities and to enable women to act as agents of their own development.
DPU (Levy) Framework	Using the core concept of the 'web of institionalisation' and adapting and elaborating various elements of the Moser framework (for example, taking into consideration the gender-related needs of men), this approach assesses the degree to which gender is institutionalised at different levels of development interventions. The main aim is to seek meaningful interchange between professionals and communities as to the most appropriate way to plan in accordance with women's and men's own needs.

Source: March *et al.* (1999)

Box 2.1: Practical and strategic gender needs

The conceptual origins of practical and strategic gender needs, now in widespread use in the gender and development lexicon, lie in the work of Maxine Molyneux (1984, 1986), who identified the ways in which policies of the Sandinista government in Nicaragua in the early 1970s often addressed only the *practical gender interests* of women, rather than their *strategic gender interests*. Caroline Moser adopted this distinction and adapted it for gender planning in the context of her 'triple roles' framework[5] by redefining 'interests' as 'needs' (see Moser, 1987, 1989, 1993; Moser and Levy, 1986).[6]

Practical gender needs revolve around the immediate, material needs of women in their existing gender roles (mainly as mothers and housewives). Programmes designed to meet practical gender needs are usually oriented to the domestic and community arena, and to the fulfilment of requirements surrounding food, water, shelter, urban services, and so on, which enable women to perform their reproductive tasks more efficiently. Since women's 'traditional' gender-assigned roles generally revolve around the care and nurture of husbands and children, the satisfaction of women's practical gender needs is likely not only to benefit women, but all members of their households.

Strategic gender needs aim to go much further than providing women with the practical means of fulfilling their reproductive roles, revolving as they do around issues of status and challenging gender inequality. As Moser (1993:39) describes:

Strategic gender needs are the needs women identify because of their subordinate position to men in their society ... They relate to gender divisions of labour, power and control and may include such issues as legal rights, domestic violence, equal wages and women's control over their bodies. Meeting strategic gender needs helps women to achieve greater equality. It also changes existing roles and therefore challenges women's subordinate position (see also Molyneux, 1984, 1986).

The distinction between practical and strategic gender needs has been increasingly taken on by agencies, and, as an example, measures identified to meet strategic gender needs in the *Commonwealth Plan of Action on Gender and Development* include equal opportunities in employment, improved land and property rights for women, better access by women to education, non-sexist education, and greater female participation in decision-making (Commonwealth Secretariat, 1995a:15).

Concluding comments

Summing up our discussion of men and masculinities in the gender policy arena, we can discern that men are beginning to feature more visibly, especially in analytical terms, than in the past. The gender relations basis of GAD approaches purportedly shifts the emphasis away from women *per se*, and opens up the field for male involvement at all levels. However, it should be stressed that this is primarily in an abstract and general, rather than substantive and specific manner. As White (1997:15) has noted: 'Mainstream development takes men's gender identities for granted, and even the move from ...WID... to ...GAD did little to shake the overwhelming preoccupation with women'. This is echoed by Harrison (1997b: 61), who comments:

Over the last fifteen years, feminist analyses have apparently influenced both thinking and practice in
international development agencies. The language of gender and development has been widely adopted. For example, awareness of the differences between practical and strategic gender needs is evident in the policy documentation of many multilateral and bilateral donors. However, the tendency for women's projects to 'misbehave' noted by Buvinic in 1985 is now replicated by the tendency of 'gender planning' to slip subtly and imperceptibly into the much older 'projects for women'. A relational approach to gender is replaced by a focus on women while male gender identities lie unexamined in the background.

One obstacle in translating the spirit of male inclusion into practice lies in the fact GAD itself is somewhat 'chaotic', with different interpretations often co-existing in the same institution. The World Bank, for example, is charged with lacking a 'common, institution-wide, rationale, common language, and clearly defined policy approach to gender and development' (Moser *et al.*, 1999:v). Although the World Bank's 1994 Gender Policy states that GAD is its framework, women are still frequently referred to as a separate target group, and the term 'gender' is often used interchangeably with 'women', the net result being a mixture and confusion of approaches (ibid.: 6; see also Färnsveden and Rönquist, 1999:86, for parallel arguments about the Swedish International Development Agency).

On the ground, too, the shift from WID to GAD has been anything but wholesale. For ostensibly practical reasons, it seems to be difficult to get away from the rather easier range of solutions advocated by WID-type policies, to embrace the greater challenges of GAD-inspired policies, which, in addition to genuine grassroots participation, stress the active collaboration of men and women in efforts to re-shape gender relations. Yet in its tendency to consign men to the sidelines, GAD in practice does not look that different from WID. This, in turn, raises questions about the utility of GAD — to women, or to men. An approach that emphasises the importance of gender relations, but seems unable to work this into practice, hovers uncertainly between theory and application, and has had seemingly limited outcomes on the ground, means that it may be time either to abandon GAD as a framework or to make a greater effort to try out some its more radical propositions.

What the development community ends up doing about gender is not the only question here, but how women (and men) might be galvanised into making the sustained effort necessary to achieve gender justice. Here the 'politics of the personal' is highly significant. One of the biggest problems with GAD, perhaps, is that it seems to have lost a lot of the (feminist) political momentum that brought its forerunner, WID, into being. Part of this has to do with the refraction and pluralisation of identity-based movements in the 1990s, but part conceivably comes from what Ines Smyth (1999:135) calls 'self-censorship' on the part of women, stemming from working with gender in development bureaucracies. Of her experience at Oxfam, for example, Smyth (1999:132) observes:

We have a Gender Policy, agreed in 1993. We write and talk about gender-sensitive policies and strategies, of gender work and gendered activities or approaches. But on feminism, feminist policies and strategies, or on feminisms, there is resounding silence.

Even if silence on feminism does not necessarily mean that people are bereft of ideals that they might still try to translate into practice (Smyth, 1999:132), it may well be desirable to invoke a more overt reassertion of feminism(s) in gender and development agendas in order to wrest GAD from some of its current dilemmas. If this is the case, then it needs to be worked out whether men can be a viable part of this process, and whether it is possible for them to be more than a mere accessory in the struggle. What is certain at this stage, however, is that even in the politically safer arena of gender and development, men are effectively only there as a figure of speech. The objective of the next chapter is to examine why.

3 Reasons for the marginalisation of men in gender and development policy

This chapter asks why men's presence as actors and participants in gender and development policy remains so limited and circumscribed after nearly three decades of 'doing gender'. Reasons offered for the conspicuous absence of men as a gendered constituency in their own right are flagged up in outline here, and explored in specific relation to case studies of contemporary thinking and practice in development organisations in Chapter 5.

Persistence of gender gaps

As touched upon in the previous chapter, one of the most important reasons for men's continued marginalisation in gender and development is that substantial 'gender gaps' remain in virtually all aspects of private and public life in every world region. Despite the growing predicament of young men who have experienced and/or participated in violence, crime, military conflict, unemployment, risk-taking behaviour, and so on, a 'crisis of masculinity' is arguably an overblown phrase to use, when seen against the evidence of women's continuing economic, political and social inequality. Although some 'gender gaps' seem to have narrowed in the last three decades, particularly in education and health (UNDP, 1998:31), the overall picture remains one of glaring difference. In the world as a whole, for example, women still only hold 10 per cent of seats in national assemblies and 6 per cent of government positions (Royal Ministry of Foreign Affairs, 1997:5). In numerous countries male use of contraception is a fraction of that of women (below 5 per cent in most cases) (Hardon and Hayes [eds], 1997). Women's average non-agricultural earnings are still only 75 per cent of those of their male counterparts, and in many countries, especially in the South, considerably less (UNDP, 1995:36-7). Bearing in mind the relative crudity of quantitative aggregate measures of gender disparities, in no country in the world is there evidence of equality between men and women in economic and political life (see Tables 3.1 and 3.2). Even life expectancy, which is generally 5-7 per cent higher for women as a result of their in-built biological advantage, is only 2-3 per cent higher in developing countries, where it has been argued that women's genetic 'head start' is prone to be 'whittled away by discriminatory treatment towards girls and women and by the risks associated with child-bearing' (Smyke, 1991:11).

In addition to the above, it is vital to note that many statistics on gender inequality do not take into account a whole range of more abstract — or less easily quantifiable — phenomena, such as the fact that women may be disadvantaged by discriminatory judicial systems, by male violence against them, by prejudicial systems of land-holding and inheritance, and so on, and by the fact that even if women have *de jure* rights, these are not necessarily *de facto* rights (Royal Ministry of Foreign Affairs, 1997:9-11). Nor do statistics show differences in power, leeway in personal and sexual behaviour, and women's continued responsibility for a disproportionate amount of reproductive labour, which shows striking similarities across a range of countries in both hemispheres (Chant and McIlwaine, 1998; UNDP, 1995).

In the light of all this, 'bridging the gap' between men and women arguably requires bringing women up to the levels of wellbeing and freedom enjoyed by the men in their households and communities, before men can lay greater claim to gender and development resources.

What's ours is ours: protecting resources for women

Aside from the persuasive case for targeting investment to women, another critically important issue in keeping men on the margins relates to the limited availability of funds for gender and development work. Although finance for gender at national and international levels has often expanded over time, the actual resources involved remain small both in absolute and relative terms (Levy, 1996:2). Faced with constrained budgets and, *ipso facto*, constrained

Table 3.1: Gender-related Development Index (GDI): selected countries, 1995

	Life expectancy at birth (years)		Adult literacy rate (%)		Combined first, second, and third level education: gross enrolment ratio (%)		Share of earned income		GDI Value
	Female	Male	Female	Male	Female	Male	Female	Male	
High Human Development									
Barbados	78.3	73.3	96.8	98.0	80.0	73.3	39.6	60.4	0.847
Singapore	79.3	75.0	86.3	95.9	66.6	57.6	31.9	68.1	0.848
Korea (Rep.)	75.4	68.1	96.7	99.3	78.4	65.9	29.2	70.8	0.826
Chile	78.0	72.2	95.0	95.4	72.1	64.7	22.0	78.0	0.783
Costa Rica	79.0	74.3	95.0	94.7	68.3	59.0	26.9	73.1	0.818
Venezuela	75.3	69.5	90.3	91.8	68.4	58.0	27.1	72.9	0.790
Thailand	72.3	66.9	91.6	96.0	55.5	49.4	36.7	63.3	0.812
Medium Human Development									
Ecuador	72.2	67.0	88.2	92.0	68.9	64.3	18.6	81.4	0.667
Iran	69.1	67.9	59.3	77.7	62.6	67.0	18.9	81.1	0.643
Algeria	69.4	66.8	49.1	73.9	62.0	66.7	19.1	80.9	0.627
Cuba	77.6	73.9	95.3	96.2	67.3	62.1	31.5	68.5	0.705
Sri Lanka	74.8	70.3	87.2	93.4	67.9	64.7	35.5	64.5	0.700
Philippines	69.3	65.6	94.3	95.0	81.8	70.9	35.0	65.0	0.661
Bolivia	62.1	58.9	76.0	90.5	63.5	65.8	26.8	73.2	0.557
Low Human Development									
Cameroon	56.7	53.9	52.1	75.1	41.0	48.3	30.4	69.6	0.455
Pakistan	63.9	61.8	24.4	50.0	27.0	53.1	20.6	79.4	0.399
India	61.8	61.4	37.7	65.5	46.5	60.1	25.4	74.6	0.424
Zambia	43.4	41.9	71.3	85.6	48.5	55.0	39.3	60.7	0.372
Bangladesh	57.0	56.9	26.1	49.4	30.9	39.6	23.1	76.9	0.342
Mali	48.7	45.4	23.1	39.4	13.9	22.3	39.1	60.9	0.229
Niger	49.2	45.9	6.7	20.9	10.7	18.6	37.1	62.9	0.196

Source: UNDP (1998, 131–3, Table 2)

Table 3.2: Gender Empowerment Measure (GEM): selected countries

	Seats in parliament held by women (%)	Female administrators and managers (%)	Female professional and technical workers (%)	Women's share of earned income (%)	GEM Value
High Human Development					
Barbados	18.4	38.7	51.2	40	0.607
Singapore	4.8	15.4	36.5	32	0.467
Korea (Rep.)	3.0	4.4	31.9	29	0.292
Chile	7.2	20.1	53.9	22	0.416
Costa Rica	15.8	23.4	45.4	27	0.503
Venezuela	6.3	22.9	57.1	27	0.414
Thailand	6.6	21.8	52.4	37	0.421
Malaysia	10.3	18.8	43.6	30	0.458
Medium Human Development					
Ecuador	3.7	27.5	46.6	19	0.369
Iran	4.9	3.5	32.6	19	0.261
Algeria	3.2	5.9	27.6	19	0.241
Cuba	22.8	18.5	47.8	31	0.523
Sri Lanka	5.3	16.2	19.4	36	0.286
Philippines	11.6	32.8	64.1	35	0.458
Bolivia	6.4	28.3	42.2	27	0.393
Low Human Development					
Cameroon	5.6	10.1	24.4	30	0.268
Pakistan	2.6	3.9	19.5	21	0.179
India	7.3	2.3	20.5	25	0.228
Zambia	9.7	6.1	31.9	39	0.304
Bangladesh	9.1	4.9	34.7	23	0.305
Mali	12.2	19.7	19.0	39	0.351
Niger	1.2	8.5	8.1	37	0.121

Source: UNDP (1998: 134–6, Table 3)

Note: Data refer to 1997 or latest available year. Countries listed in descending order of HDI score.

18

choices as to how to allocate funds, it is perhaps not surprising that women have continued to be a priority target group. Indeed, given the historical record of gender-blind and gender-neutral approaches,[1] if women are not targeted specifically it is questionable how they might fare in respect of access to any development expenditure at all.

One of the biggest questions which emerges from discussions about integrating men and masculinity into gender and development work is whether this would reduce the pool of income allocated to women. As noted by the International Planned Parenthood Federation (1998:56), for example: 'A major concern in this issue of male involvement is whether funding for women's reproductive and sexual health will be reduced in order to meet the reproductive needs of men'. A more cynical take on calls for projects for men could be that this panders to 'the "backlash" against feminist pressure for gender equality' (UNESCO, 1997:5). Moreover, even if extra resources were to be made available for 'men and gender', this would still create competition for funds which are already scant, in an era of shrinking budgets for aid and social expenditure around the world.

Considering the finance issue from another angle, however, we have to recognise that keeping men out can, in many respects, be just as limiting as bringing them in. This is because a discernible 'vicious circle' whereby continued tendencies for 'gender' to be equated with 'women', and for the formulation and implementation of gender initiatives to be carried out by 'women's offices', means that prospects for capturing a larger share of development resources are limited. This is, perhaps, especially true given the prevalence of male personnel in gate-keeping positions in umbrella organisations, and the difficulties of engaging men's support for gender equality, either within development organisations themselves (as discussed later), or in grassroots communities.

The trouble with men: gender conflict at the grassroots

Aside from concerns about sharing resources, the desire among gender and development personnel to retain a primary focus on women, and in many cases to proceed with women-only projects, stems from fears about the consequences of what opening the doors to men might bring. These fears revolve around anticipation of net losses for women, including a reduced profile and visibility for women and women's concerns, the hijacking and subversion of women-oriented projects, and the dilution of feminist struggles.

Regrettably, these fears can be regarded as legitimate: there have been numerous cases of development initiatives in which men and women have participated, and conflict has surfaced between them, often remaining unresolved. Examples at the grassroots are legion. These range from men's difficulties in conceptualising patriarchy as a system, as discussed by Kamla Bhasin (1997) on the basis of her involvement with men's workshops in various parts of South Asia, to the practical and operational difficulties of male–female co-operation in housing and community development projects (Fernando, 1985; Vance, 1985). Indeed, even where initiatives have been explicitly and primarily gender-oriented, it seems to have been difficult to prevent men from 'taking over' or to achieve any substantial change in gender relations. For example, a drive on the part of Oxfam to introduce 'gender-aware' development in Western India was seriously challenged by the difficulties of gaining men's support for women's projects. The predominantly male leaders of low-income communities in the region recognised that they would have to respond to Oxfam's gender initiative in order to continue getting funds, but reconciled their dilemma by devising some very traditional development activities for women that would remain under men's control (see Mehta, 1991). Other common examples include micro-credit programmes, where loans to women have ended up in men's hands, and/or led to growing indebtedness among women (see Goetz and Sen Gupta, 1996; but see also Kabeer, 1998, for a different perspective). If these are common outcomes of including men at the grassroots, then it is no surprise that women in development agencies have been cautious about expanding such initiatives further.

The legacy of WID in gender and development

At the broader level of gender policy formulation, an additional explanation for the omission of men stems from the origins of present-day gender and development teams and units in a global (if not unified or unilateral) struggle for the advancement of women's rights. Although, as we have seen, some WID approaches are less radical than GAD approaches, they were nonetheless motivated by a desire for gender justice, and pressed by people who were themselves active in feminist movements (Pearson, 1999). Even if some of the most extreme political demands were lost, when early WID campaigners swelled the ranks of 'femocrats' within the international development system (ibid.), it is unlikely that all feminist goals were sacrificed, notwithstanding that something of a veil of silence fell on feminist questions in organisations in the 1990s (Smyth, 1999). Similarly, even if official WID programmes and institutions that emerged during the 1970s and 1980s tended to be more conservative than popular women's and feminist movements, they continued to be informed by them, besides which their specific mandates were to address women's issues. Although 'feminism' now covers a much more refracted range of movements than in the past, and the term 'feminisms' is often substituted to do justice to the increasingly widespread and vocal movements of women in the South, women's rights and empowerment remain a guiding spirit for many workers in the field. As such, despite the terminological shift from 'women' to 'gender', and the fact that 'gender' and 'feminism' are not synonymous (Smyth, 1999:139), the legacy of WID's emphasis on women has undoubtedly been a factor in keeping men at bay.

Resistance to GAD in development organisations

Added to the above, another block to men's inclusion emerges from the fact that WID has tended to prove much more popular among major development agencies than has GAD. There are technical and political dimensions to this, which are often interrelated.

One highly important obstacle, flagged up in the previous chapter, is that gender and gender relations often prove very difficult to treat in a planning context. Although there might be considerable theoretical support for the notion that gender is complex and differentiated, translating this into practice is often beyond the limited time and resources of development agency staff who, in Harrison's words need 'a kind of conceptual shorthand — "simple principles" and "methodological tools"' (Harrison, 1997b:62). Regrettably, however, as Harrison goes on to point out: 'In the course of such simplification,

recognition of the potentially contentious and inherently political (as opposed to technical) aspects of gender relations is usually the first to go' (ibid.) . A related problem with GAD is that it requires a much longer and, *ipso facto*, larger commitment of resources, where the ultimate aim is to re-shape inequalities grounded deeply in local cultures.

Emerging out of this last point, another major stumbling block to GAD is the way in which gender is often deemed a threat to the diplomacies of development interventions. As Eva Rathgeber (1995:207) comments:

The social relations of gender are labelled as falling into the realm of culture and strong advocacy for a rethinking of gender relations would be seen as unwarranted 'cultural interference'.

Resistance to intervening in gender in the development mainstream derives from a supposed respect for cultural relativism, notwithstanding the rather large contradiction posed by the fact that development itself is a Western construction and imposition. Moreover, other inequalities based on class and income, which are just as contentious, are often seen as fair game among outside agencies (Mehta, 1991:286).

While a palpable distaste for heavy-handed interventions in other people's gender arrangements can also be seen as arising from the growing discomfort among women in the North about the imperialism of forcing Western feminisms on Third World women (see Smyth, 1999), another long-standing reason for the traditional preference for WID over GAD is that, while the former is essentially a non-threatening, 'add-on' approach to women and development, GAD calls for much more fundamental and integrative strategies, which have been often perceived as 'confrontational' (Moser, 1993:4; see also Parpart and Marchand,1995:14). Indeed, even within the WID paradigm itself, it is obvious that a desire to avoid major change or conflict has worked to make certain approaches more popular than others (Buvinic, 1983). Naila Kabeer (1994a:7), for example, argues that the WID anti-poverty approach arose out of difficulties of taking on the 'bold women's agenda' inscribed in the WID equity framework:

In view of the resistance by predominantly male-staffed redistributionist concerns, equal-opportunity pro-grammes, even in their watered-down versions, presented high political and economic costs which undermined their chances of implementation. Instead, the new focus on women was accommodated within the official agencies of development by linking it to the emerging concern with poverty alleviation and basic needs.

The patriarchal culture of development organisations

A third set of factors which have contributed to the lack of incorporation of men and masculinity into gender and development are concerned with what Longwe (1995:18) terms the 'patriarchal culture of development agencies'. Just as concepts of patriarchy and masculinism are embedded within traditional development approaches (Scott, 1995), the organisational structure of development bureaucracies continues to be decidedly male-biased. Men still vastly outnumber women in the upper echelons of donor organisations, and they have done little to advance the gender agenda (Jahan, 1995:130-3; Lotherington and Flemmen, 1991; Rosario, 1997:83). Coupled with male dominance in national governments in the South, this has meant that feminist principles and values do not just go against the grain of agencies' internal norms and traditions, but '... also stand in the way of cosy and comfortable alliances with the patriarchal governments of the Third World' (Longwe, 1995:18). In short, these clusters of 'men on top' have presented a formidable obstacle to GAD, let alone a GAD approach that aims to work as actively with men as it does with women in challenging unequal power structures. Even with the relatively safe option of women-oriented GAD, Longwe's (1995) inspired analogy of the 'patriarchal cooking pot' reveals numerous overt and covert strategies adopted by the development mainstream to obstruct progress. These include keeping resources to a minimum, diversionary action, verbal trivialisation, and ineffectual procedures for organisational change (ibid.). Staffing stands out as one of the most obvious examples, where, through keeping women out or confined to specific 'women's departments', the force for advancing women's strategic gender interests is kept to manageably low levels. As noted by the International Planned Parenthood Federation (IPPF) (1998:6):

The path to women's genuine power-sharing in many organisations is riddled with examples where women were appointed as 'tokens' on Boards and Committees without any real power, or where under-qualified women were promoted with the expectation that their failure or ineffectiveness could justify not promoting other, perhaps more qualified, women.

This observation is echoed by Caren Levy (1992:135-6), whose discussion highlights the wider consequences of rendering gender policy and planning a 'male-free' zone.

... the last 15 years has seen the creation of a narrowly-based women's sector, manifest in the creation of 'women in development' offices in international agencies, funding ministries of women's affairs and women's bureaus, implementing women's projects with women's groups. One of the most disturbing features of this 'women's sector' is that it is a weak sector. It is characterised by a lack of any real political influence, and is therefore underfunded and under-staffed, both in numbers and qualifications. A key factor underlying these characteristics is the conceptualisation of both the problems and the strategies of this sector in terms of women, not gender. A focus on women is recognised as legitimate in its own right and the basis of one of the most important political movements of the century. However, when translated into professional practice over the last 15 years, it has resulted in a sector which is marginalised from mainstream development policies, programmes and projects, with little impact on overall development processes and economic, social and political relations in many countries (emphasis in original; see also Goetz [ed.], 1997; Kabeer, 1994a; MacDonald,1994).

Although there is no intention here, nor is it appropriate, to portray all men in development organisations as antagonistic to the aim of gender equality, the fear that women's empowerment can threaten male entitlements has undoubtedly been a major issue (Kajifusa, 1998:5).[2] In addition, it has been widely argued that disinterest and resistance often flow from men who 'feel that "gender" has nothing to do with them' (Cornwall, 1998:53). One plausible reason for this is the long-standing entrenchment of male privilege and power, which leads men to be less likely to see the social relations of gender as problematic (Rathgeber, 1995:207). One interesting finding from a pioneering study of men's participation in the promotion of gender equality in the Swedish International Development Agency (SIDA) was that male staff perceived the organisation to be much more gender-equal than their female counterparts did (Färnsveden and Rönquist, 1999:59). Men in SIDA also had much more self-confidence about their knowledge of gender issues than women gave them credit for, and also believed in their own abilities to be successful in their tasks (ibid.).

The idea that gender is not a problem or priority is perhaps particularly pertinent to senior men in large national or international development bureaucracies, who benefit from having power not only over women, but also over other men. In turn, more junior men, whose promotion and prospects depend on peer validation, may avoid raising gender issues for fear of disapproval or ridicule. They are possibly even less likely to press a *male-inclusive* gender agenda, if this would involve shared and honest self-reflection among their colleagues. Whether or not this is so applicable to NGOs, with their generally 'flatter' management structures, is another question (though see also below).

Aside from fearing what other men might think, men who might be sympathetic to GAD in some respects, may at the same time be resentful about how much of a role they can actually play in determining the way in which it is approached by their organisation. Despite GAD's emphasis on the importance of gender as a relational construct, and on the theoretical importance of incorporating men, the terms on which men and male concerns are included in GAD do not tend to be set by men, or even by mixed groups in many cases, but by women. Accepting female *dictat* may not sit well with men who have first got to come to terms with problematising power relations among themselves, and who are likely to be grappling for a script that presents an appealing, and feasible, alternative to that embedded in conventional male socialisation. The tact and sensitivity that is needed in addressing these issues is not always evident, as so aptly illustrated by the title in the Cairo Programme of Action on Population, on the 'Empowerment and Status of Women versus Male Responsibilities and Participation' (Shepard, 1996:11). This kind of language is hardly likely to get men rushing headlong to join the queues at contraceptive clinics or to change their sexual behaviour. In a similar, but more general vein, Feleke Tadele (1999:35) points out that:

Men will find it difficult to work on gender issues if women assume that men should be working for their own immediate loss of power, as women gain power. Instead, both women and men need to be persuaded that gender equity would mean the equal participation of men and women in decision-making.

Reminding us that although gender prejudice is usually seen as a 'peculiarly male problem ... women's gender prejudices can be just as blinding' (Cornwall, 1998:46), the unfortunate tendency for gender analysis to ignore the diversity of male experience and interests, and to tar all men with the same brush, may make those men who would like greater involvement feel there is no point in trying.

Men in the 'GAD ghetto'

For men who are employed in gender and development departments, there may be other reasons for unwillingness to promote a greater role for men. One factor is temerity about pressing men's agenda for fear of falling out of line with the usual emphasis on women (Kajifusa, 1998). Another obstacle is that male personnel may not have been accorded any space in which to raise new issues. Here, for example, it has been levelled by men that debates on gender within institutions have often not been as 'open' as they might be. Lack of debate on gender clearly closes down opportunities for men to be included as clients, as well as collaborators:

Open and honest debate at the organisational level should encourage men to gain more than a superficial commitment to gender issues. With a greater intellectual conviction of why and how gender equality can and should happen, men will not merely be encouraged to change their attitudes towards women and towards themselves (which we increasingly understand as necessary), but will build on this knowledge in their own lives, We can make allies among men who will then behave in a gender-sensitive way when 'unsupervised' and act as advocates for change among their colleagues, family and friends (Roche, 1999:206).

A third factor which makes men unlikely to be the prime movers in introducing men and masculinity on to the agenda of gender and development is that they may not want to take the credit for advancing a struggle led by women, and over which women are often extremely, and understandably, proprietorial. Moreover, if they do succeed, this may be taken as evidence that male authority is needed to make things happen, and so provoke resentment among their female colleagues.

Perceptions of men's interests and privileges

Last, but not least, it is highly plausible that, in light of men's generally privileged position in society in general, and in the development arena in particular, it is taken for granted that men's interests are already catered for, thereby precluding the need for specialised provision. The eloquent and economical statement, 'After a millennium for men, we got a decade for women',[3] expresses concerns that are deeply felt by many people in the gender and development community. As articulated in a report for UNIFEM on the gender-differentiated impacts of macroeconomics, for example, Corner (1996:72) asserts:

The interests and concerns of men are automatically incorporated in development policy and planning because men are the decision-makers. Economic theory represents a man's view of the economy because most economists are men and the system that determines appointments, publications and promotions in the discipline rewards those that espouse such a view.

Leading on from this, it may well be surmised that men are in a stronger position to advance their interests than women, and that involving men will merely perpetuate traditional patterns of male supremacy. As Goetz (1997:17) points out:

... 'men's interests' are presumably just as difficult to identify objectively as women's, nor is the category 'men' any more valid as a universal than is the category of 'women'. The historical record, however, does show that men tend to act across divisions like class or race more cohesively than do women in defence of certain gender interests, and they do so in ways which mean that public institutions help to forge connections between men's public and private power.

When it comes to thinking about men's specific *gender needs*, it is often conjectured that these will revolve around a desire for self-preservation and the maintenance of inequality. However, this denies the fact that, like women, men are a differentiated group, and may well have diverse objectives according to class, stage in the life course, ethnicity, and so on. Men may also have some common interests, such as in the realm of health-care (Beall, 1995a), or in challenging their exclusion from certain domains of activity, such as child-care (Levy, 1999; March *et al.*, 1999:124). To date, however, these concerns have been overshadowed by the fact that men have most of it their own way most of the time, and, given this legacy and the systems that have developed to uphold it, they cannot be trusted to play fair.

Concluding comments

In identifying the reasons for the continued marginalisation of men from gender and development, it is clear that there is a plethora of positions ranging from the conscious to sub-conscious and overt to covert. In some instances, it is possible to see men as having been deliberately left out of the picture; in others, that this may have happened unwittingly; and in others, that although the will might be there, enforcement has been weak due to the costs, time, and labour involved in intervening in the complex terrain of gender relations.

Two factors stand out as particularly important here. One is a question of what might be called 'fair deals', by which we refer to the idea that preparedness to include men in gender and development might well have been more advanced by now if women had been allowed an equal place and say in development in general. Given the common tendency for gender policies to evaporate within the 'patriarchal cooking pot' (Longwe, 1995), and the incontrovertible evidence of continued disparities between men and women in the world at large, there seems to be a stronger case for continuing to press for women's mainstream 'agenda-setting' (Jahan, 1995) than for concerning ourselves about a small (and effectively sole) area of development planning in which men have been left out, and often with good reason.

A second factor is that it may be the case that until a gender-relations approach is piloted to a greater degree, and there is solid assurance that this will not cancel the (albeit limited) gains made by women over the last 30 years, men may have to give women a larger share of the limelight. Here, considerations of gender equity as well as gender equality are vital. Although the latter may at the bottom line be a question of balancing numbers, the former refers to a sense of 'fairness or justice' (IPPF, 1998:13). In relation to reproductive health for example, the IPPF (1998:56) notes that since women usually take on a larger share of the burden of reproduction in respect of costs, dangers, and burdens (physical, mental, social, economic, and so on), ' ... it is equitable and fair that women should have a greater share in the decision-making' (ibid.:13). So, too, perhaps, should this be the case in the wider field of gender and development, which, without women, would probably not have come into being at all.

4 Including men in gender and development: principles and rationales

Our review thus far indicates that views on gender and development, let alone men and masculinities, are far from uniform, and that the prospect of consensus on policy goals and strategies remains elusive. Nonetheless, it is conceivable that more dedicated attention to men, and to their greater incorporation into gender and development at planning and project levels, may ultimately benefit women and further the cause for gender equality. With this in mind, this chapter raises a series of arguments that in hypothetical terms might justify men being brought more squarely into gender and development policy. The chapter is divided into two sections. The first highlights reasons why the exclusion and/or marginalisation of men may be detrimental to gender and development initiatives (especially in the beneficiary capacity). The second outlines key gains that might be achieved by giving greater priority to men at grassroots, operational, and policy-making levels.

Male exclusion as detrimental to gender and development

Stereotyping and its discontents

Although not exclusively to do with omitting men, but with the more general problem of failing to engage with the socially-constituted dynamic nature of gender relations, a major problem of equating gender with women is that it can contribute to stereotypical treatment of women and men alike. Gender stereotypes in Northern development agencies have frequently been criticised as essentialist, monolithic, heterosexist, imperialist, and degrading, to both women and men in the South. As summed up by Cornwall (1998:46):

All too often in development ... women are treated as an identifiable single category, thought of in a narrow range of stereotypical ways. 'Men', equally thought of as a single category, lurk in the background, imagined as powerful and oppositional figures.

A further observation, by Kabeer and Subrahmanian (1996:8), is the pattern of depicting gender relations as 'unchanging and unchangeable':

Biological determinism — particularly the remarkably wide tendency to attribute certain roles and tasks to women and men on the basis of some notion of 'natural' suitability — is one form taken by this attempt to eternalise *gender inequality* (ibid.; emphasis in original).

One of the major results of a static view of women is that they are rarely perceived as individuals in their own right, but first and foremost as wives and mothers. The tendency to assume that women's concerns are 'family concerns', and that women are uniquely positioned to act as conduits for the delivery of resources to other household members, is not only pervasive, but gives rise to the belief that women can extend their domestic responsibilities on an unpaid basis to the broader realm of community projects (see for example, Beall, 1995a; Chant, 1995b).

Following on from this, it is no surprise to find women and men lumped into the dichotomous categories of 'good girl'/ 'bad boy' stereotypes, wherein women are represented as 'resourceful, caring mothers', and men as rampantly selfish individualists (White, 1997:16). Quite apart from drawing a veil over the fact that '... differences within the notional interest group "women" may be just as much of an obstacle to collective action as differences between women and men' (Cornwall, 1998:50), women are routinely constructed as a 'vulnerable group', universally oppressed by their menfolk. This not only denies women agency, but casts men as the 'villains', or at the very least, 'the problem'. Aside from the fact that excluding men gives them little chance to challenge the constructions imposed upon them, dealing with 'the problem' *through* women, negates the self-reflection on the part of men that might be crucial to change in gender relations. It also burdens women with a task that arguably needs to be shared rather than shouldered single-handedly. Another outcome is the tendency to emphasise that men routinely benefit from development. This is dangerous, not only because it 'naturalises' their power (Kajifusa, 1998:11), but because '... not all men ... have power and not all of those who have power are men' (Cornwall, 1997:11).

Leaving men out of the picture not only fails to engage with the *processes* that construct gender identities and so often result in women 'losing out', but also neglects aspects of gender, including war, violence, and AIDS, which, though relating primarily to masculinity, adversely affect everyone, as discussed later in the chapter.

Alienation and hostilities

Leading on from the above, another common set of consequences of leaving men out revolves around male alienation. Exclusion is hardly likely to be an effective means of achieving rapprochement, and in many cases may aggravate hostilities. Indeed, there is much evidence to suggest that men do retaliate when excluded and that this can severely prejudice the success of gender initiatives.

One example here is provided by the experience of PROCESS, a Filipino grassroots NGO with origins in the women's movement and a strong participatory agenda. In the early 1990s, PROCESS started running women-only seminars in gender-awareness and women's rights for wives of male trade union members in a big mining plant in the Central Visayas. Because they had neither been informed nor invited to the seminars, some of the men demanded that the organisers either let men into the meetings or give up running them altogether (Chant, 1995b).

Another analysis, of women's income-generating projects in Greece, Kenya, and Honduras, undertaken by Constantina Safilios-Rothschild (1990), showed that projects aimed at raising women's access to income in situations where men have difficulty being breadwinners were often unsuccessful. Men facing pressures of long-term employment insecurity would respond to what they regarded as 'threats' posed by improvements in women's economic status by taking over projects, controlling the income women derived from them, and/or, as a further backlash, increasing their authority and control within the home.

Clearly there is a question here about whether such backlashes arise because men are not involved in specific projects, or because of more general anxieties revolving around the fragility of their livelihoods and status in the light of rising unemployment. It is likely, however, that both sets of factors have a part to play.

More work for women

Aside from deliberate responses on the part of men to being 'left out', male exclusion can lead to bigger labour burdens for women. With reference to the work of Folbre (1994) on gender and parenting responsibilities, Sweetman (1997:2) identifies that a focus on women alone can lead to 'overload and exhaustion'. This is echoed in research on Costa Rica, which suggests that the increasing emphasis in social policy on women heads of household can actually drive men still further from assuming responsibilities for care of dependants (Chant, 1997b). The idea that male exclusion results in overload for women is even more pertinent where 'efficiency' considerations have guided gender and development initiatives.

Widely linked with the neo-liberal market-oriented policy framework that accompanied the debt crises of developing countries in the 1980s and 1990s, the efficiency approach is interested in harnessing women's purportedly 'under-utilised' labour to cushion low-income households from the consequences of neo-liberal macro-economic reform, such as cut-backs in public expenditure, rising prices, declining wages, and falling levels of male employment. The efficiency approach aims to make development more efficient, and assumes that women's increased economic participation will lead to increased equity. Yet while some practical gender needs may be fulfilled by targeting women, such interventions are often observed to result in women working for development rather than *vice versa* (see Blumberg, 1995:10; Elson, 1989, 1991; Kabeer, 1994a:8; Moser, 1993:69-73). Moreover, age-old assumptions about women being mothers and housewives, and having the capacity to extend their working day in the interests of others, mean that gender inequalities may be intensified as a result (Andersen, 1992:174; Chant, 1995b). For example, UNICEF-endorsed programmes aiming to protect basic health and nutrition, such as the *Vaso de Leche* (glass of milk) and *Comedores Populares* (popular kitchens) schemes in Peru, draw heavily on women's unpaid labour. By capitalising on and reinforcing the under-valuation of female labour, this does little to redress gender inequalities (see Moser, 1993:73).

The limits of 'women-only' projects

Last, but by no means least, lack of male involvement can also mean that benefits of women-only projects in general may be limited. One of the most important issues here is the limited advancement of women's strategic gender interests. In the PROCESS example cited earlier, for instance, although women claimed to have enjoyed the seminars on women's rights, the benefits were limited by the fact that they could not exercise the rights they had learnt about in their own homes (Chant, 1995b). Conceivably, male involvement might have made men more sympathetic. In a similar vein, the first poverty-alleviation programme for women household heads established by the Figueres administration in Costa Rica in 1996 had arguably less impact than it would have done if it had included men. Despite proposals for a male-inclusive 're-socialisation of roles' component in the programme, this was dropped on the grounds that it would be too difficult to execute. Instead, workshops on rights, self-esteem, and so on, were restricted to women, who still had to deal with unsensitised men in their personal lives, and with patriarchal structures in both the private and public arena (Budowski and Guzman, 1998). The limitations of placing the onus for change on the 'victims' were felt so deeply by some women that they actually asked local organisers of the programme if their menfolk could participate (Chant, 1997b).

At a more pragmatic level, excluding men can place a responsibility on women that they are unable to fulfil. In the field of health, for example, Wood and Jewkes (1997:45) note that ignoring men belies misplaced assumptions about women's ability to 'control their bodies and thereby achieve and sustain sexual health'. Such assumptions are perhaps particularly serious as far as HIV/AIDS is concerned, since women continue to be vulnerable to infection due to forces beyond their personal control. As Foreman (1999:xi) notes:

Attitudes towards sex are in a state of flux almost everywhere, but in many societies men are still expected to have frequent intercourse with their wives or regular partners and occasional or regular intercourse with their casual partners. Women are expected to accede to men's demands, abstinence is seen as harmful, and condoms are seen as unmasculine or as restricting a man's pleasure. As long as men — and women — are influenced by such concepts of masculinity, HIV will continue to spread.

Another example relates to the exclusive targeting of women in nutritional training schemes. Although women in many cultures may have the main responsibility for food provision, it needs to be recognised that they cannot necessarily determine the dietary behaviour of other household members. If men are excluded from such projects, they may not perceive the need for new diets and, if they refuse to change their eating habits, women's training will come to nothing (Wallace, 1991:185).

For a number of reasons, therefore, it could be advantageous to include men, as explored in more detail below.

Rationales for male inclusion at the grassroots

Relevance, responsibility, and the benefits for women

Women rarely operate as autonomous individuals in their communities and daily lives, so programmes that take into account, and incorporate, male members of their households and neighbourhoods may well make interventions more relevant and workable. Indeed, in practice it is entirely possible for men to be allies, as evidenced by UNICEF-supported women's farming groups in Luapala province, northeastern Zambia, where male membership was justified by women on the grounds that they needed the men, and could not see any reason why men should not take part (Harrison, 1997a:128-9).

Even where male–female relations may be less co-operative, active efforts to engage men in gender projects can help not only to dismantle gender inequalities, but to make men bear greater responsibility for change. For example, the pilot project of ActionAid's 'Stepping Stones' (a training package designed to address HIV/AIDS awareness, gender issues, and communication and relationship skills among young men and other community members), held in Uganda, resulted in a decline in domestic violence and alcohol consumption after 16 months of participation (Large, 1997:28).

The process of getting men to realise the worth of changing gender relations that oppress them, and challenging them, may also not be so difficult as anticipated, if it is emphasised that empowering women does not necessarily mean disempowering men (Kanji, 1995:4). Moreover, given the fact that men as well as women have problems with 'gender culture' (White, 1994:108), it is by no means beyond the realm of possibility that men too will benefit from interventions that question the immutability of gender roles and relations, and that involve them in the struggle for justice. Reinforcing a point made in the previous chapter:

... prescribed masculine gender roles constrain men: they often restrict men's role in childrearing, nurturing and caring roles. This is men's loss as these roles, if shared, can be rewarding ... Men have a great deal to gain, not just power to lose in re-negotiating/transforming gender relations (Metcalf and Gomez, 1998).

Indeed, research in Cali, Colombia, has shown that where men have been forced into joining women's home-based micro-enterprises as a result of declining opportunities in the wider urban economy, they 'spend more time at home than before and develop new skills and aptitudes as parents and in household chores' (Pineda, 2000). Such changes have frequently led to more equitable and harmonious relations between spouses, in which new forms of masculinities can emerge and flourish. For this reason, Pineda stresses the importance of more comprehensive gender policies, which draw lessons from the grassroots, cease to neglect men, and conceive of women's empowerment in such a way as to free it from the notion of a 'zero-sum' game in which women only gain at men's expense (ibid.).

Aside from the potential to reduce gender inequalities, and to foster more equal relations between individual women and men, there could also be wider benefits from male inclusion. In the field of family planning, for example, Judith Helzner (1996:5) argues:

A number of goals could be served by changes in patriarchal male-female dynamics: the social justice objective of increasing equality, the demographic objective of lowering population growth rates, and the public health goal of reducing disease, especially sexually-transmitted infections. Greater participation by men could thus contribute to the goal of reproductive health in a variety of ways.

Last but not least, bringing men in could mean that gender transformations will be more sustainable.

Men's rights as human rights

Leading on from the above, in terms of the post-Beijing GAD Equality approach, to deny men the rights that women have (or technically should have) in gender and development is effectively in breach of human rights principles. As Large (1997:29) points out:

Gender as an area of research and action should be understood as belonging to men and studies of masculinity, as well as to women and feminist studies.

A rights-based strategy may well work to the benefit of everyone, not least for instrumental reasons. As Shepard (1996:12) asserts with reference to reproductive health: 'Stating that men have a right to care for their children, for example, offers an entirely different approach to the male target audience'. Nonetheless, there is also disquiet about this, with Sweetman (1997:6) concerned that:

... advocates of human rights could legitimately question the way men are being co-opted into health debates as 'instruments' to deliver a development goal. This uncomfortably echoes the way in which women have been used as an instrument to deliver population control in the past. Ultimately both men's and women's rights to determine their own lives are compromised by this.

By the same token, it should also be noted that women's human rights have often been seen as separate from general human rights, with the consequence that these have often been unobserved, and their violation unexposed and unchallenged (Tomasevski, 1993). In many respects it could be argued that men remain a privileged group in this area, and that until more is done to equalise gender-based inequalities, greater effort should be targeted towards enabling women to secure the basic rights and freedoms enjoyed by most men.

Men in crisis?

A possibly more convincing reason for including men in gender and development is that many men seem to be experiencing such major, rapid, and disquieting changes in their lives, that a 'crisis of masculinity' is in evidence. Although the exact nature of this crisis and *whose* crisis it really is needs much greater scrutiny, what is certain is that men are more *uncertain* (Chant, 2000b). As Foreman (1999:21) puts it: 'In a world in which masculine values no longer provide the security that they seemed to provide for their fathers and grandfathers, men's fear is growing'. It is increasingly the case in a range of contexts that young men are 'the ones at the bottom of the heap' (Cornwall, 1998:46), with low-income and working class men being most affected (Barker, 1997). As Silberschmidt

(1999:173) notes in relation to the traditionally male-dominated society of the Kisii District, Western Kenya, ' ... today men are left with a patriarchal ideology bereft of its legitimising activities and not able to fulfil new roles and expectations'.

Yet among the several reasons in the 'world out there' that make it timely to address men in gender and development, is precisely the changes that have undermined 'traditional' masculine identities which have effectively opened up a space to imagine new futures. In the realm of parenting, for example, Engle and Breaux (1994:37) suggest that the moment has come to stop ignoring fathers, to 'recognise the social and economic situation we all share, and find ways to weave a new social fabric out of the broken strands of worn-out stereotypes'.

Another very important reason to tap into current trends in men's 'predicament' is that it could be dangerous if steps are *not* taken to intervene, not least for women and children. Castells (1997:136), among others, observes that individual and collective anxiety over the loss of male power is provoking increases in male violence and psychological abuse. Alcoholism and marital strife are also on the increase (Barker, 1997; Silberschmidt, 1999). UNESCO also notes that where men lose power and status and are unable to enjoy their routine entitlements, women may be the main victims:

Where men have economic advantages over women, they have a privilege to defend, which may be defended with violence, or may make women vulnerable to violence. Economic changes which put at risk or destroy men's traditional livelihood without providing alternatives, makes violence or militarism attractive options (UNESCO, 1997:6).

Aside from the potential spin-offs for women, men's suffering is worthy of attention in its own right. In many areas of the world, including Eastern Europe and urban Latin America, men are beginning to bear a greater burden of ill-health than women, though this is not for the same reasons as women, but more to do with 'lifestyle' factors, such as road accidents, work injuries, and cardiovascular illness (Barker, 1997:5-6; Jiménez, 1996). Men's sexual behaviour is a major factor, with sexually-transmitted diseases such as HIV/AIDS spreading in large part from unprotected sexual liaisons (Campbell, 1997a). Morever, men are currently 80 per cent of the 6-7 million injecting drug users worldwide (Foreman, 1999:128).

Last, but not least, there are signs that men themselves are seeking for help:

Worldwide, men largely derive their identity from being providers or 'breadwinners', and lack ideas, or alternative gender scripts, to find other meaningful roles in the family in this changing economic environment. Research worldwide reports that men are confused about their roles in the family and about the meanings of masculinity in general and are requesting opportunities in which to discuss and deal with these changes (Barker, 1997:4).

Renegotiating masculinity

Aside from arresting some of the processes arising with men's transitions in the late twentieth century, a more male-inclusive approach to gender and development carries with it the potential of renegotiating 'masculinity' as well as redressing gender imbalances. Recognising that 'masculinity' is not something exclusive to men (Cornwall, 1997), and that as opposed to being 'given', it is something 'rather fragile, provisional, something to be won and defended, something under constant threat of loss' (White, 1997:16), its prospective amenability to change should be regarded as positive. This is especially the case for those men who suffer domination, discrimination, and violation from other men, and who are unable to live up to the social ideals prescribed by 'hegemonic masculinity' (Quesada, 1996:47), a concept defined by Robert Connell (1987:186) as constructed in relation to women as well as subordinated masculinities, closely connected to the institution of marriage, and decidedly heterosexual. Nowhere is this truer perhaps than in situations of armed conflict, as Large (1997:25) has noted: 'Men may be unwilling to participate in acts of violence, yet the social relationships in which they are caught up pressurise them into complicity' (see also UNESCO, 1997:6).

As Foreman (1999:14) summarises:

Masculinity brings with it privileges and, in many societies, freedoms denied to most women. Such privileges, however, impose burdens, with many men having sex and refusing condoms because they are conditioned to do so, rather than because they want to. Furthermore, subconsiously, some men resent the obligations imposed on them; that resentment is often manifested in anger and violence towards women and other men.

Rationales for involving men in gender policy and planning

As we have seen at various stages of this document, male-inclusive gender and development is not just about bringing men in at the grassroots, but also about engaging them at institutional levels. Among the various reasons why this could be beneficial in theory, a crucial factor is that men can have an important influence on other men. In various cultural contexts, men are more likely to listen to men, including when it comes to talking gender (see for example, Tadele, 1999). Using men for gender-related work is increasingly being recognised as a strategy for change, particularly in the domain of reproductive health. In Bangladesh, for example, where the immense power of male religious leaders has often turned men (and *ipso facto* their wives) against the use of contraception, the government has attempted to educate religious leaders about the benefits of family planning in the hope that this will influence take-up rates (Neaz, 1996).

Aside from the desirability of bringing more men into gender work at operational levels, building a critical mass of gender-sensitive men within development agencies could have a domino effect, and work towards the destabilisation of patriarchy in institutional cultures (Chant, 2000a). This in turn could mean, in the longer term, greater resources for gender and development and more sustained institutional commitment to the continuing reduction of gender inequalities (Färnsveden and Rönquist, 1999:85). Without men on board, it is unlikely that this can happen. This is not just about capitalising on reserves of male power in the development establishment, but is also a question of equity. As Foreman (1999:35) has suggested: 'The challenge of the future is to create societies where women's strength achieves its full potential without relegating men to insignificance.'

Concluding comments

In this review, we have tried to bring out some of the key reasons why men might be accorded more space in gender and development policy and planning than they have had up to now. Although we have drawn on some case study examples in the analysis, our main concern was to evaluate the arguments in principle. How viable some of these propositions have proved in practice, and how they might be put into operation, forms the subject of our two remaining chapters.

5 Including men in gender and development: practice, experiences, and perspectives from development organisations

Introduction

This chapter reports on the results of interviews (conducted primarily in the United Kingdom and the United States) with 41 specialists in development and gender questions, representing nearly 30 organisations, agencies, foundations, and consultancies, which are involved in international WID/GAD projects (see Appendices 1 and 2). The themes discussed in this chapter — largely concerning sectoral issues such as health and sexuality, violence, education, employment, fathering, and issues affecting young men — emerged as core concerns of the persons we interviewed. In some areas, such as sexuality, there appears to be enough experience and conceptual clarity to begin to draw significant lessons. In most other areas, however, our interviews indicate more a desire that work should begin around issues like fathering, for instance, than truly substantive accomplishments to date.

Of the 33 women and eight men interviewed for this report, all but three or four individuals expressed a strong desire for involving men in GAD work. That said, fewer than ten individuals were able to describe actual work done with men by their organisations. Further, nearly all people consulted conveyed serious concerns regarding how men should or should not be 'brought on board'.

It is also worth noting at the outset that of the literally hundreds of pages of transcripts generated from the interviews, there was remarkably little of direct relevance to men and development. This reveals the minimal work with men that has actually been conducted. Nonetheless, it was also strongly apparent in the interviews that even in conceptual terms, the issue of involving men in GAD elicited a considerable divergence of opinions. We have striven to accurately represent this diversity in this and the following chapter. The last thing needed is for simplistic solutions to be offered to the multiple obstacles and problems inherent in 'men-streaming' gender. What is clear, however, is that many of the arguments about the advantages of encouraging men's engagement in GAD work have emerged from the 'bottom up': several of the individuals consulted noted that the move from WID to GAD was already occurring at the grassroots. This had led officials in organisations to begin thinking about broadening the scope of their analysis and activities as well. Kate Metcalf, of the International Education Unit in ActionAid, for example, talked about the involvement of men representing a *'post hoc* response' to what was being demanded in the field, pointing out as well a greater awareness of this need in the South than in the North. Naana Otoo-Oyortey, of the International Planned Parenthood Federation (IPPF) in London, cited 'donor pressure to include men', which had taken at least ten years to filter up to the higher echelons of development agencies.

At the same time, of course, men have always been involved in policy-making, and within the operational leadership of development work, and most people interviewed emphasised this. Rabiya Balewa of Abantu for Development in London noted: 'Men are there; they've always been there. Men have been controlling development for God knows what. Men have been enacting policies. Men have been changing policies at will.' While a secondary focus of this report is the 'involvement' of men in development agencies themselves — in project design, implementation, and review procedures — the fact is that men have not very often been included as participants in WID/GAD programmes for all the reasons detailed in Chapter 3, including the commitment to focusing on lessening inequalities suffered by women, limited funds, and fear of men hijacking feminist goals and projects.

As was made clear in all the interviews conducted for this report, distinguishing between men as a generic, abstract category, and the part actual men play in relation to gender inequality, is complex and controversial. Therefore, determining how to mainstream men ('men-stream' in our epigram for Chapter 1) in GAD work is both a question in its own right and one intimately connected to the overall issue of mainstreaming gender in development work. We see value in maintaining a distinction between men and gender (and women and gender, for that matter) — and not just as analytical distinctions — precisely because, as was underscored in the interviews, the question is not simply when to include men and how, but also when *not* to include men and how *not* to do so.

And, again, it is worth emphasising the *de facto* nature of 'men's involvement' in development: as administrators, opponents, and facilitators of projects in the guise of husbands, fathers, and sons. Men have always been present in some form to neglect, dismiss, encourage, or simply observe women's activities related to development. What is novel, then, has to do with involving men intentionally and directly, as gendered persons in their own right, and because they are involved in socialising others into gender roles and identities.

Health

Reproductive heath and sexuality

Programmes in reproductive health and sexuality have been transformed globally in recent decades through local and regional feminist and gay movements. These political campaigns have both signalled and intensified the impact of the widespread availability of effective and low-cost birth control, which, in turn, has altered the nature of sexuality in many respects, as pregnancy is now no longer necessarily the outcome of heterosexual sexual relations. Today, sex and sexuality are less tied in the minds of millions worldwide to 'nature', and more than ever viewed as part of the map of gender relations, rather than biological imperatives.

The history of development work around reproduction and sexuality began with women. Yet as Judith Helzner, Director of Sexual and Reproductive Health at the IPPF, Western Hemisphere Region, remarked:

I think a lot of scholars and activists started out talking about only women and then actually saw — from the perspective of the success or failure in real world attempts to change things — that you can't deal with just women in isolation. The idea of change in a system means that both women and men have to change for there to be a real difference. Our work on male involvement in reproductive health and family planning evolved out of the work focused on women.

In 1992 the IPPF approved as one of its key objectives:

To increase men's commitment and joint responsibility in all areas of sexual and reproductive health and sensitise men to gender issues, as an essential element in ensuring women's equality and an enriched couple relationship for both men and women (IPPF, 1993:17).

Echoing the views of the IPPF and other organisations in the field, Ann Leonard, in the International Programmes Division of the Population Council in New York, stated in her interview:

The reality is that it's women — not elitist women, but grassroots women — who want this. They want their partners involved. We're developing a vaginal microbicide, and the thinking was that women would want to use this product clandestinely, as something they could use without telling their husbands. And when we first went to Zimbabwe to test it, women said: 'We have to tell our husbands. They have to know what's going on.' Otherwise they have all kinds of problems. That surprised people.

Similarly, Eliza Mahoney of AVSC International (not an acronym) in New York discussed, in our interview with her, the 'Men as Partners' programme in South Africa, explaining that the instigation for it came 'from clients coming to us and asking us to talk to their partners'. She explained:

I think family planning clinics have created an important space for women in which they have autonomy and information and education, which they may be lacking in other areas of their lives. I think that's been very important. Unfortunately, we've ignored the context in which they live. We haven't thought about what happens when they leave the clinic, return home and men are still the primary decision-makers no matter what.

In reference to development work on reproductive health, Oxfam GB, in particular, has cautioned against 'seeking only to change the response of male partners to "yes" regarding contraception and disease prevention', insisting that development projects should also emphasise 'the valuable understanding which is gained by looking at the relationship between women and men' (Sweetman, 1997:6).

Through the experience of involving men in discussions regarding sexuality and reproductive health, development workers have learned about the potential for change both among women and men. Marilyn Thomson, Gender Adviser at Save the Children in the UK, reported on the basis of experiences of talking about these topics with male youth in Somalia:

31

So the younger men were saying, 'I don't want to marry a woman who's been infibulated', and they'd really been moved by this discussion, because nobody had ever thought of sitting down and talking with them about it.

In a broader consideration of reproductive rights programmes in Mexico and other regions, Juan Guillermo Figueroa Perea (1998:1) writes:

It is not too much to say that the medicalisation of fertility regulation, supported by sexist processes in analytical interpretation, standard-setting and the pursuit of greater demographic impact, has discouraged male involvement in the processes of reproduction.

The relation of such medicalised and sexist processes to recent figures for vasectomies worldwide should require little elaboration: Helzner (1996:15) reports that in 1992, an estimated 41.5 million men had been sterilised, compared with nearly 140 million women.

To compound the programmatic difficulties regarding methods to involve men in reproductive health work, there are, to date, relatively few ethnographic, epidemiological, or demographic surveys with respect to male fertility.[1] Indeed some demographers have declared the topic unmeasurable, which is one reason that ongoing debates on male fertility are valuable. The scattered evidence throughout the world pertaining to a diverse array of practices associated with men and fertility remains to be synthesised statistically and ethnographically. Many report higher rates of spousal abuse during a woman's first pregnancy, for instance. At the same time, and perhaps not entirely unrelated, little systematic investigation has been conducted on related issues such as men's role during a partner's pregnancy and men's presence and participation during childbirth, men's attitudes and behaviour in relation to abortion, and so on.

Another area of sexuality that has received great attention, though not always under the WID/GAD umbrella, relates to AIDS and sexually transmitted diseases (STDs). As mentioned in Chapter 4, programmes aimed at men engaged in heterosexual relationships such as Stepping Stones in Uganda have had an impact not only with respect to AIDS, its primary target, but also corollary problems such as domestic violence and alcohol abuse. As for the general inclusion of men who have sexual relations with women, Helzner of the IPPF, New York, maintained in our consultation with her that:

You could treat a woman every day for a sexually transmitted disease and, if her partner has it and doesn't get treated, too, then he just keeps reinfecting her. So in epidemiological terms, it doesn't make sense to keep wasting medication on women if you don't treat men, too.

It is also true that despite the supposed conceptual and programmatic broadening of development work from WID to GAD, and in addition to the question of whether or not to include men under the rubric of 'gender', there are not only tendencies to separate women from men but also, with respect to sexuality, to consider only heterosexual men. Deborah Rubin, Economic Growth Adviser of WIDStrat (Women in Development Strat Project) stated pointedly in our interview:

I have questions about the whole construction of this [World Bank-funded] project, because I think that in some ways it's taking us back a step to a more biologically reductionist notion of what gender was meant to move us away from.

Nothing in this report, we trust, will serve to construct impermeable categories of men and women, because beyond these labels we would emphasise the need to incorporate feminist and gay-studies theories regarding gay men, bisexuality, and what are often referred to as 'third genders and sexualities' (see Herdt, 1994).[2] That is, although we do see the continuing need to have special programmes for men and women (see Chapter 6), our conceptual understanding of gender and our overall programmatic context for GAD work is rooted in the relational power-dynamics between men and women, and, in the case of men addressed in this report, between different men, some with more and some with less power for reasons of class, ethnicity, age, and other social factors (see Box 5.1).

Violence

The Puntos de Encuentro group in Nicaragua sees itself as 'swimming against the current' in developing programmes and workshops among men to prevent male violence against women (Montoya, 1998). In Nicaragua, as elsewhere, men are reported to be increasingly confronted with problems (from their perspective) stemming from women's independence and assertiveness. Talking about work in India, among other countries, Helen Pankhurst, Head of International Programming for Womankind Worldwide, reported:

For the men, they value the fact that we are working on the economic stuff. But we get problems for the fact that we're working with empowerment, and there is an increase in violence generally [as a direct result of these recent changes].

Throughout the world, laws and penalties are becoming stricter, and therapy and assistance for women and children are growing. The scarce resources available that are being used are going first and foremost to help battered women and their children, though there are some innovative programmes underway. In her interview, Andrea Murray, Head of the British Council Gender Team, mentioned a project in Pakistan in which 'male Pakistani gender trainers work with male police officers around issues of domestic violence'. More is surely needed. Clearly, as Katherine Wood and Rachel Jewkes (1997) write in a paper on rape and

sexual coercion in a South African township, these efforts among women are simply the short-term solution to a problem which, by definition, directly implicates men.

In Latin America, three out of four young people who die from violence are male (Figueroa Perea, 1998). Male-gendered violence, meaning violence by men directed at men — often motivated by homophobia — as well as violence by men directed at women, provides a separate set of data for which reliable statistics are rarely available (see Schifter, 1998). The issue of men and violence is further complicated because, although men and masculinity are clearly implicated, gender research has long since discarded an early cultural feminist analysis that universally equated men with violence and women with peace. As discussed in Chapter 4, the fact that adolescent males throughout the globe are recruited as cannon-fodder in wars and other

Box 5.1: Salud y Género in Mexico

In 1992, the NGO Salud y Género (Health and Gender) was formed by health workers, including some with an additional background in anthropology, to work on health-promotion efforts. Today, Salud y Género operates offices in two medium-sized cities in Mexico (Xalapa and Guanajuato), and conducts workshops throughout the country. The organisation started working with women initially. Fairly quickly, women began demanding that training be done with men. Now, counsellors and trainers work with groups of men, groups of women, and some that combine both men and women.

As to how men might be included in health projects that focus on women, Benno de Keijzer, the founder of Salud y Género indicates:

What we tell programmes is that they need to at least take men in to account and find ways to block resistance or at least ease it, so that women have more opportunities to participate in activities that empower them. I think work with men can be preventative in many ways. It is important to protect battered women and children, for example. I think you have even better prospects if you can work with grown men and youngsters to prevent this violence in the first place and when you do simultaneous work with young girls and young women to build self-esteem and assertiveness.

The two major areas of work of Salud y Género today are (1) advocacy around public policy and (2) training on issues of health education, gender, and development. Benno de Keijzer explains that in Salud y Género workshops, for example:

…we talk with men about the general theme of masculinity, and how certain hegemonic traits of masculinity carry a heavy cost on the lives of the men themselves, in terms of their health and their fathering, for example, to say nothing of the costs for the women in their lives.

Trainers try to pick up on particular topics — like violence, consumption of alcohol, sexuality, fatherhood — and work through the gendered aspects of the practices, that is, how they are conditioned by being men.

In terms of broader public-policy advocacy, Salud y Género uses occasions like Father's Day to work with the media to raise awareness of gender equity and responsibilities, and the pleasures as well as difficulties of parenting. Another is a 'white ribbon' campaign among men to show their opposition to violence against women.

Source: Interview with Benno de Keijzer, Lima, Peru, 9 June 1999.

armed conflicts is a reflection of particular social and cultural dislocations rather than some essential, testosterone-driven proclivity toward violence on the part of young men.

Similarly, while several of the people interviewed employed the term 'machismo' to characterise male practices in areas as far apart as East Timor, West Africa, Zimbabwe, and Latin America — thus utilising what has become the international code word for domineering men — we suggest that rather than generalising in this fashion about men throughout history and across the continents, we would do better to analyse the specific contexts in which gender relations persist, are reproduced, and are transformed (see Gutmann, 1996). As Lorraine Corner, Head of UNIFEM-Bangkok, maintained in her interview: 'In a sense you are always shooting yourself in the foot when you ignore the gender dimension of men's violence'.

Other health concerns

The statistical relationship between men and mortality and morbidity is generally acknowledged as showing disproportionate levels of accidents, cases of HIV/AIDS, abuse of alcohol and other drugs, suicide, and violence, as well problems relating to lung cancer, prostate cancer, and cardiovascular problems. There is far less solid research and applied work on the relationship of *masculinity*, or, rather, different masculinities, to all these health problems. Why indeed men die on average earlier than women is a matter of some considerable debate. Although, as pointed out in Chapter 3, women purportedly have an in-built genetic advantage, it cannot be denied that masculinity constitutes a risk factor (see Foreman, 1999; de Keijzer, 1998). To date there is little evidence of widespread experience in GAD work in relation to male use and abuse of alcohol and other drugs, except perhaps as they represent a drain on household finances. Until these and other unhealthy practices commonly associated with men and masculinity are changed, it will be difficult to settle this debate.

A key area of concern, if one involving less extensive experience, concerns men and mental health. From taking seriously questions pertaining to male subjectivity — in relation to suicide, for example — to the task of counselling men who have been witnesses and victims of violence and sexual abuse, to dealing with stigmas associated with homosexuality and 'homosociality' (social bonds between men and

men), to clarifying differences based on ethnicity which are sometimes mistakenly attributed to mental disorders, psychological issues involved in work with men and masculinity are significant, despite the fact that they are often veiled behind more overt social crises such as wife-beating and alcoholism. As Debbie Rogow, independent consultant, identified in her interview: '... work with boys ... clearly documents the enormous ways in which their ability to have access to an emotional life and an emotional language gets shut down. And how painful that is for them.'

Those interviewed for this report seemed clear on the need to take seriously the question of men's affective relationships, for example, but beyond improving lines of communication in development organisations themselves, most were less sure what this meant on the ground for projects and programmes.

One of the key justifications given by many of our interviewees for working with men in GAD concerned the need to prevent numerous health-related problems before they became serious challenges. Aside from evidence that men are more reluctant than women to seek medical care until it is 'too late', unless routine work is done with men on questions of domestic violence, for example, GAD work in this area can hope for little more than *post hoc* healing and protection of battered women. Prevention efforts among men are in their infancy, yet there is some positive experience, such as the work on violence done by the Puntos de Encuentro group in Nicaragua, and outreach in Nigeria involving the Alhaji Tijani Lawal Traditional Healers clinic on the subject of family planning (see IPPF 1996b:17).

Education

Phil Evans of the Social Development Division of DfID, UK, argued in his interview with us that: '... the big headline-grabber was when the [World] Bank claimed that education for girls is the best investment you could make to reduce poverty'. Yet although there is ample evidence pointing to continued male bias in literacy and educational achievement (see Chapter 3), and very distinct regional and local experiences with respect to education, there are signs of change. For example, Lorraine Corner of UNIFEM-Bangkok reports that, whereas in Bangladesh and Pakistan, girls' and women's access to education remains much more limited than it is for their male counterparts (Corner, 1996:51), in our consultation with her, Dr Corner observed that in Mongolia, girls were attending junior high school in larger numbers than boys. This trend at secondary and/or tertiary levels is also documented for certain Caribbean countries, including Barbados and St Vincent and the Grenadines (Chant and McIlwaine, 1998), for Cuba (Lumsden, 1996:120), and for Mexico.[3]

Shaha Riza, a Gender Specialist with the Middle East and North Africa Region of the World Bank, related the following experience in our interview:

In Morocco, for example, you see more and more boys dropping out of school or never going to school at all. I think this is an issue. It's not just a PR issue to make the men in the [World] Bank notice gender and that there are problems with women as well. This is an issue that has an impact on the whole development project. You have more boys dropping out or never attending school, basically because of economics.

Gabriela Vega, a Social Development Specialist with the Inter-American Development Bank (IADB), reported in her interview that in indigenous communities in Bolivia, Guatemala, and Mexico, even where girls were matching boys in terms of school enrolments, the problem of girls participating less than boys was far from settled. There are a few areas in which wide disparities favouring females over males in education have been reported; for example, Sharon Robinson of the Commonwealth Foundation stated that getting boys to go to university had recently emerged as a 'big problem'. However, as Vega stressed, attendance is not the same as taking part, and, more importantly, attendance is not the heart of the issue about men's involvement in this aspect of GAD work.

The crux of the matter, in the view of several people in our survey, is the *content* of education; in particular, non-sexist, non-homophobic training of girls and boys. Unless boys are thought to be inherently the way they are from birth, the ideas and practices associated with various masculinities in the world are a matter for debate and change, including via formal educational systems. That is, we know that girls learn certain things in school, or not, and GAD projects have consistently attempted to emphasise issues such as the need for girls to become more assertive. That there is a related set of gender concerns that may be addressed to boys is obvious. Further, such educational standards and programmes must, as always, be carefully designed so that fundamental concerns regarding ethnic differences are not ignored in an effort to regiment homogeneous 'male' and 'female' instruction.

Employment

Considering that employment encompasses such an enormous proportion of development work in general, it is worth noting the paucity of experience or even thinking in the development community regarding men's gendered relationship to employment questions. Corner (1996:59) sums up this concern by saying: 'The entry of women into the manufacturing workforce has been one of the most widely researched gender-related aspects of the impact of export-led development in Asia and the Pacific', and this is undoubtedly true of other regions as well. In addition, whereas the fact that women still work longer hours for less pay in many parts of the world is widely described in the development literature, there is virtually no research or programme work devoted to the impact on men, as men, of the economic transformations of recent decades, such as those involving shifts to 'flexible accumulation' and the like (see Harvey 1989). A number of our interviewees also emphasised that the issue of employment is one in which links between class and gender, and a host of related social divisions such as ethnicity and age, may, and should be, made explicit.

For example, in many societies in which poverty-alleviation programmes and women's participation in micro-enterprise efforts have been underway for several years, men's status as breadwinners has been roundly challenged, with severe repercussions for both men and their families. Vijayendra Rao, an economist at the World Bank, described the ramifications of a programme in South Asia:

For instance, in a micro-credit programme, there's some evidence that men are using women as a conduit for bringing resources into the family. And there's resentment that only women can bring resources to the family. In a programme I was involved in six to seven years ago, men would ask, 'Why isn't there anything for me?' 'Why is there only help available for the women?' And these are valid questions. They didn't have access to credit, but we were giving it to women when the men were better educated and perhaps in a better position to take the information we provided them and be productive. There was a lot of confusion about what it was we were trying to do and there were a lot of conflicts that arose inadvertently.

From the legal realm of work and inheritance laws to escalating conflicts in the domestic sphere as women not only work more than men but sometimes earn more as well, male familial and social contributions are being questioned as never before (see Chant 1997a: Chapters 5 and 6). Linked to changing kinship relations and marriage patterns, some research points to strengthened extra-marital ties — for example, with brothers as an important source of external support for women (see Fonseca, 1991) — as well as certain advantages enjoyed by women-headed households as they diverge from traditional models (see Chant, 1985; González de la Rocha [ed.], 1999).

Some of the implications of the gendered impact on men of recent changes in employment patterns and the role of development agencies in this respect will be discussed in the final chapter of this report.

Fathering

Based on their work in rural areas of Mexico, including with indigenous populations, Benno de Keijzer and the group Salud y Género have found that fathering often provides a window through which to involve men in a host of other programmes related to masculinity, including health and education (see de Keijzer, 1998). These findings are confirmed in some (limited) GAD work with fathers elsewhere in the world.

Judith Helzner of IPPF New York reported in our interview: 'People find that fatherhood is a major selling point for work with men in our [reproductive health] field. They may not want to put a condom on, but they might like a better relationship with their sons and daughters.' Beyond extending the meanings of fatherhood to incorporate more than procreation, Gabriela Vega (IADB) discussed in her interview that work with men around fathering can involve more than simply men's activities with their children in the home. In particular she pointed out that, just as women have become engaged in school-related efforts, men may be drawn into activities related to their children's formal education.

Several people interviewed suggested that the entire literature that has developed on intra-household decision-making and conflicts should be utilised to gain a better understanding of the

gendered qualities inherent for both men and women. Around the issue of child-care, for example, although this is sometimes presented as a problem for women alone, the issue of affordable and convenient day-care is, or should be, a pressing issue for fathers as well. Sree Gururaja, in the Gender and Development Intersectoral Cluster of UNICEF in New York, noted in her interview that as a result of her organisation's recent efforts to emphasise men's roles as caregivers with children, they have found that 'men nearly everywhere express a desire to be better fathers'. Thus, this is a 'good entry point' for the involvement of men in development work generally.

And where men are not concerned about such matters, this too implies the need for GAD work with men. In the pioneering 1997 issue of Oxfam GB's journal *Gender and Development* (reprinted as a book in the Focus on Gender series) which focused on men and masculinity, published by Oxfam UK, Caroline Sweetman, the editor, insists:

Continuing to work with women only — for example, targeting female-headed households as beneficiaries of funds earmarked for 'gender and development' — has allowed development organisations to side-step the uncomfortable issues associated with 'interfering' in relations between men and women within the household (Sweetman, 1997:2).

Patrice Engle (1997:31) adds to this discussion by noting that 'social service and health programmes continue to target mothers and children, ignoring the role of men in the lives of children'. Clearly, questions ranging from abandonment of families by men, to custody issues in cases of divorce and separation, are related to social and cultural practices associated with masculinity and fatherhood in a particular society. Development work is needed which supports men as fathers, to enable them to meet the various demands made of them ranging from supporting their children economically, to supporting them emotionally. If this does not occur, development policy and practice will be obliged to continue its current focus on salvage operations which aim to enable women to bring up their children alone.

Young men

For numerous reasons it is clear from our survey that young men represent a group requiring special attention in the overall effort to involve men in development. In our interview with Marilyn Thomson of Save the Children, for example, she discussed a film project on masculinity involving film-makers from India, Nepal, Bangladesh, and Pakistan:

They're doing films on what it means to be a man and masculinity in their own countries. We had a process with them participating in workshops so that they could look at common identity issues. The idea of the films is to work with young men, so that the film will go with the handbook which will suggest points for discussion and so on. And also with young women as well, but the main focus is on young men and the whole question of their perception of their masculinity.

Ann Leonard of the Population Council in New York stated in her interview that:

I think men and adolescents have been missing. Especially from the family-planning perspective, they really have been left out of the equation. And the problem is that since 1994, and Cairo, when there was an official 'OK', that, 'Yes, we ought to be looking at men more', for a lot of people that translated into contraception. Now it's OK again to target men. Or, 'Men are the decision-makers, so let's get men to decide whether their wives should have family planning', which is a real concern if you've invested your efforts in trying to get women some autonomy over their own bodies.

In a study of adolescent fathers in Chile, sociologists José Olavarría and Rodrigo Parrini (1999) call attention to the need for social recognition of and attention to teenage sexuality among males as well as females. They point out, for example, that in Chile young men are excluded from programmes for teenage mothers, thus reinforcing not only stereotypes of negligent fathers but erecting institutional obstacles to teenage men assuming responsibilities early on in the lives of their children (see also the discussion of the programme for female household heads in Costa Rica in Chapter 4). Olavarría and Parrini also point out that, in Chile and other societies, little scholarship has methodically investigated adolescent male sexuality and the relations adolescent fathers have with the mothers of their children and with pregnant girlfriends and wives, despite this being a common popular concern in these countries (ibid.).

Based on a nationwide study in Kenya regarding determinants of male fertility and sexual behaviour, it is reported that 63 per cent of men interviewed had first sexual intercourse between the ages of 15 and 19 years, while 27 per cent had sexual intercourse before the age of 15 (IPPF Africa Region, 1996:28-29). Many men interviewed in this survey demonstrated ample knowledge about family planning; the fact that they chose not to use birth control in many cases demonstrates that knowledge is insufficient to determine practice. Further, the study argues, men appear to make many and perhaps most of the decisions regarding contraception, a fact that points to the importance of including young men in family planning work (ibid.). Also in Kenya, Naana Otoo-Oyortey of the IPPF London told us in our interview:

There is a project going which looks at men — the 'other half', basically — and clinics have been set up for men, just men, to look at male needs. A couple of programmes are going to address the issue of men's active involvement within women's sexual and reproductive health.

In addition to these particular questions and needs of young men with respect to sexuality and reproduction — and others related to HIV/AIDS and STDs — several of those interviewed for this report note the prevalence of young men in statistics pertaining to unemployment and crime, homicides, vehicular accidents, alcohol abuse, as well as State-sanctioned and society-wide instances of organised violence. How to make practical connections between these sectoral issues for young men was of concern to many in our survey. For instance, Marilyn Thomson of Save the Children discussed her organisation's success in this respect through the use of a video in a workshop linking issues of violence and HIV/AIDS to the general question of masculinity.

'Men only' sanctions and stigmas

Once again, on the issue of men and development, when discussing the benefits and liabilities of promoting activities and forums for 'men only', it is important to recall that in many respects and venues development work has long been an exclusively male domain. The experiences and opinions of GAD workers throughout the world are indeed contradictory with respect to organising training sessions for men only, recruiting and utilising men only as trainers, and targeting men as a separate group for work around any aspect of gender and development.

In Nairobi, there have been men-only family-planning clinics, such as Kencom House, since 1993, just as in Ghana in the 1990s development workers began to organise lectures and group discussions about family planning at work places throughout the country (see IPPF 1996b). A Young Men's Clinic, whose clientele is largely Dominican migrants, opened in New York City in 1986 (see Armstrong *et al.*, 1999). Based on their efforts in different international contexts, the IPPF administrators whom we interviewed each argued strongly for male-only forums for discussion of reproductive health matters, as the best means of reaching and influencing men's thinking and behaviour.

Diversity among men along class, ethnic, regional, and generational lines also requires flexibility in programme planning, so that questions of racism and homophobia, for example, are adequately addressed and in order for men to have ample opportunity to air their views and fears. Indeed, while some of those interviewed seemed inclined to ridicule the cliché about men not being able to cry — implying that this was of little importance — others seemed intent on finding ways for GAD to aid men in discussing male subjectivity, men's affective experiences and worries.

There is still too little practical familiarity with the dynamics of gender training to know what difference male trainers may make. Although, as discussed in Chapter 2, what limited evidence there is suggests that men's awareness of themselves as gendered beings may be raised if gender training is led by 'gender-sensitive men', we must also recognise that this is likely to be highly context-dependent. Counselling sessions for men who have abused their wives in Mexico City attended by one of the authors of this report were routinely led by women, with no apparent reluctance on the part of men to discuss issues of masculinity or violent behaviour. On the other hand, according to many of those whom we interviewed (including Helzner of IPPF New York, Leonard of the Population Council New York, Metcalf of ActionAid in London, Otoo-Oyortey of IPPF London, and Rogow), very often men prefer to have male counsellors, and men are best able to open up to and confide in male trainers.

One obvious issue with respect to any activities involving 'men only' has to do with control of the finances. In order to combine women's supervision with a male only environment, groups such as ReproSalud in Peru have designed their programmes for men so that the original feminist gender orientation of the organisation is maintained by devolving to women the ultimate decision-making with respect to all important aspects of funding and organisation of workshops and other programmes. Addressing similar concerns, Helen Pankhurst of Womankind noted in our interview with her:

By putting our resources with women to make that decision about how they think men should be supported is a very useful change to 'Let's just work with men and women together'. Letting women say how they want to work with men is much healthier.

As for development organisations themselves, the issue of male involvement not simply in general but specifically in GAD work is rather stark: indeed, why *aren't* men demanding to get into gender work? According to Gabriela Vega of IADB:

Men haven't formed a group to promote 'men in GAD' because they've taken the reactive role, and not the proactive one. The reactive role has been to be scared or aggressive towards the women's movement. And, in the worst situation, indifferent.

Discussing the same theme of finding ways to recruit men into GAD work, Chris Roche, Head of the Programme Policy Team in Oxfam GB's Policy Department, spoke in a more personal vein:

The challenge has to be surely how you enthuse people for something that goes to the heart about all those debates about society, about the roles in reproduction, caring, bringing up kids, fatherhood … This issue is so critical to so many facets of people's lives. It isn't a marginal issue. It's central.

And, as in other aspects of exploring the question of men and development, there was considerable disagreement not merely with respect to the feasibility of interesting more men in development work, and how to accomplish this goal, but whether it should be a goal in the first place. Most important of all, however, was the expression of resounding concern on the part of our respondents that men should not be allowed, once again, to take over this aspect of development.[4] Additional factors were that staffing is not simply a matter of individual (or institutional) ideologies: questions of promotion, parental leave and support, and interpersonal relations were held by most people to be central concerns involved in transforming GAD from marginal to mainstream in development work overall. Nonetheless, although men being involved in gender work is routinely marginalised in organisations as a whole, particularly those not centrally focused on GAD work, it is also true that men may receive extravagant praise for their minimal participation in work that many women have been diligently labouring through for decades.[5]

Perhaps in development organisations, as out in the field, a lesson may be learned from the women in South Asia about whom Kamla Bhasin (1997:55) writes: 'Rural women said they were now quite aware of women's issues, and it was time that their men were given a proper 'brain-wash' (*dimaag dhulai*).'

Concluding comments

Summarising on the basis of our survey with individuals representing more than two dozen international governmental and non-government agencies and organisations devoted to questions of poverty, reproductive health, and development, it is clear that there is tremendous interest in finding ways to incorporate men in GAD work generally. Nonetheless, it is also plain that few practical efforts have been made along these lines, and that there is a tremendous need to clarify 'terms of engagement' as well as specific policy goals that lead to greater involvement of men-as-men in development projects.

Briefly put, as Kate Metcalf insisted in her interview:

It's not just enough to change women. We need to change men as well, and analyse masculinity and challenge it. That, and femininity, as well. I think that the aim would be to bring men into feminist [gender and development] work. There's been that debate in the feminist movement on whether to allow men in. Because they take over and all of that. But in the end I think it's going to strengthen [GAD work], getting men on board and kind of taking them seriously.

Nearly all those interviewed for this report expressed the desire to involve men in GAD work. Nearly all, as well, seek to accomplish the goal of integrating men in initiatives around reproductive health, violence, employment, and more besides, under the rubric of feminist conceptual frameworks and leadership. Without bringing men on board, GAD work is potentially hobbled, according to both those we interviewed and, through them, numerous women clients throughout the world, since women are left as the only people responsible for transforming gender relations. Without retaining links with feminist politics, involvement of men runs the risk of detracting from, rather than supporting, pre-existing GAD work. In the concluding chapter we will address initial proposals as to how men may be brought into ongoing and new development projects within a variety of feminist perspectives.

6 Moving men from obstacles to collaborators: many rivers to cross?

Introduction

In this chapter we highlight the main conclusions of this report, regarding reasons for and against involving men in development work generally, and we present suggestions for initial efforts that might be made to accomplish the goal of GAD, incorporating men and male gender issues in a fashion that furthers the feminist goal of equality between women and men. We believe there is work now that can, and should, be done to involve men in GAD. At the same time, we caution that there are no magic answers and that this involvement should occur carefully and systematically. As the interviews we conducted for this report make clear, there is a need to include men and women together in some projects, as well as simultaneously maintaining separate projects and goals for women. The practical suggestions offered towards the end of this chapter seek to utilise the most innovative work (for instance, in reproductive health) to date, and to indicate some new areas in which efforts to involve men in GAD work might be channelled.

The concept of including men in development is certainly clearer than the practical matter of attaining this goal. As we stated in Chapter 2, and as demonstrated more clearly in the preceding chapter, there are few guidelines for men's involvement in GAD. In addition, concerns about using men as 'window-dressing' and women as a 'smokescreen' for inactivity in confronting fundamental gender inequalities are all too real. If we view men in their gendered and gendering qualities, then involving them in development work represents still less charted territory. When we distinguish between men as agency chiefs and men as husbands, fathers, sons, and grandfathers, it is not because there are no gendered qualities in each grouping, but in order to stress that something *has* been missing from GAD work to date: men as a gendered group. Men as managers of development projects are in a radically different position regarding gender inequalities from men who are in low-income families, for reasons including class privilege and power. Whatever conceptual insights offered by

them, bland pronouncements about 'patriarchy', 'machismo' and the like often prove less than useful in practical efforts to transform the actual conditions and relations of inequality.[1]

Among the major limitations of the present study is the fact that, with few exceptions, we did not have the opportunity to consult Southern NGOs/development agencies. Of those representatives of organisations and individual consultants whom we were able to interview, there was general, though far from uniform, consensus that GAD in practice still means WID; and that, flowing from this, in relation to gender and development work, apart from a smattering of men in the organisations themselves, men are formally little involved at the grassroots in the programmes and other activities of these organisations. There is, nonetheless, some positive if scattered experience from which to draw lessons and at least a modicum of inspiration.

Men as a human category have, as we have repeatedly emphasised, always been present, involved, consulted, obeyed, disobeyed, and so on, in development research, policy, and practice. Yet, men have rarely been acknowledged to be a gendered category, and have rarely been drawn into development programmes that seek to promote gender equality, in any substantive way. While most of the representatives we interviewed feel that more work with men should be done under the GAD umbrella, there is less consensus on how, and how far, this should go. Existing disagreements may simply stem from different understandings of what is meant by 'including men'; for example, several interviewees felt strongly that, in a real, if narrow, sense, 'men' had always been involved in development work as managers and recipients of funds, for example, and thus it made no sense to them to discuss 'men and development' as anything new, interesting, or necessarily good. Unquestionably, even with greater conceptual clarity, challenging debates will and should continue over the virtues and risks of involving men in GAD work. As Ramya Subrahmanian of the Institute of Development Studies, Sussex, UK, noted in a personal communication:

In India it's clear that the most transformative processes that are sustainable are those led by women themselves, where the women find the means of including their men in the process. They don't want to lose their husbands and male supports, and hence they find ways of striking balances and trade-offs. They are the best experts on male inclusion in a sense.

Among the approaches to involving men in development are two very different extremes: one, in which questions of power and inequality are central to GAD; the other, in which it is emphasised that men, too, suffer, albeit in different ways perhaps, from gender divisions, and that men's narrower interests provide the best basis upon which to involve men in GAD. The views of the authors of this report have affinities with both approaches, and particularly with the first, since, as Caroline Sweetman of Oxfam GB has put it: 'Men and masculinity need to be studied if power relations between the sexes are to be changed for the better' (Sweetman, 1997:2). As Helen O'Connell, the Education and Policy Co-ordinator of One World Action, told us in her interview:

I think it's really positive that there is a strong push now to looking at men. For political reasons it's vital, and for practical reasons, as well. Because we all know stories about how projects have been undermined because men have been excluded from them.

Uncharted territory — no fast tracks

To put our priorities squarely forward first: there is undoubtedly a real threat that the push for involvement of men-as-men in GAD work might lead some managers and directors to withdraw money from programmes previously earmarked for women. This should not be the way that men are brought on board. Men should be involved in GAD only if extra resources are allocated. If more funds are not available, in our view it would be better to leave things as they are for the time being, than to take money away from present projects aimed at women, regardless of WID/GAD nomenclature. As argued by Sweetman (1997:6):

Development policy-makers need to be clear on their reasons for focusing on men and male gender issues, ensuring that this work is seen as additional work on gender issues which does not divert resources away from addressing the interests of women.

The study of men and masculinities in both academic and development settings, inspired in large measure by feminist scholarship and advocacy, is in its infancy. Regardless of widespread popular opinions on the subject, we can rely on little systematic knowledge of men and their beliefs and practices as gendered human beings. For this reason alone, the process of involving men in GAD work is likely to be slow. Despite the force of our recommendation that changes are needed, and that men must be incorporated far more than they have been in GAD work, we also urge caution for all the reasons spelled out in earlier chapters of this report. As noted by Simon Maxwell, Director of the ODI, on the one hand, 'The big challenge is to get the gender people out of the ghetto'. On the other hand, the perceived and real threat of 'men taking over' must be acknowledged, managed, and averted. To quote Naana Otoo-Oyortey of the IPPF in London: 'Our emphasis is not so much on men but addressing men as partners, and addressing men such that men are not going to take over.' There are plainly numerous potential problems of involving men in GAD work, including that pointed out by Suzanne Kindervatter, Director of Interaction: 'A possible negative implication would be if "men in GAD" re-establishes male favouritism in families'. The key strategic challenge will continue to be to find ways to utilise women's expertise regarding how and when to involve men in GAD, and how and when not to do so.

Certain sectors of GAD work have a long-established and secure feminist orientation, such as the reproductive health field. Perhaps reproductive health may represent one of the key areas for future research and planning to test the waters for including men in GAD work. In addition, as in other areas such as those related to double standards of education, divorce, and the diversity of male identities and practices along ethnic and other lines, with respect to reproductive health, sexuality, and questions such as abortion, there may be a greater ability in GAD work to utilise the mass media to help disseminate information and promote campaigns.

With respect to other areas such as employment and credit, which have long tended to be male enclaves exhibiting reluctance to include women, it may be less feasible early on to involve men in GAD work. At the same time, work in this sphere is important, as Lorraine Corner of UNIFEM Bangkok made clear in our interview with her:

41

If you look at the early microcredit programmes in countries like Bangladesh, when we go back and look again we begin to realise that because the men were just sort of ignored, then often the project totally failed to reach its objective. The women repaid their loan, sure. But what did they repay it from? From working harder, from selling their daughters, from whatever, because the man actually took the money and used it for his own purposes. Because she has so little power and so little control in the family, that realistically it was never an option that she was going to be able to control it.... Clearly you have to involve the men in some sense.

Corner added later, in the same interview:

If you look at countries like Mongolia, you know there's still very much a WID approach that says, 'We're doing very well. 70 per cent of our borrowers and micro-enterprises — and this is not even a WID project — are women.' Or 80 or 85 per cent. And I think, 'My God!' What I hear is that women are supposed to bear the entire economic burden in this society. What are the men doing? And the answer is that the men are frustrated; their traditional gender roles have been largely destroyed. And they're driving themselves to drink and beating up their women in the process.

The image of mainstreaming, or 'men-streaming', can be useful here in imagining how to involve men in GAD work. As we write in Chapter 1, streams can either be well managed or ill managed, but regardless, they are going somewhere and generally to larger bodies of water. In our view, it is unwise to ignore these currents, and better to chart and tame them as best we can.

Ways to test the waters of male involvement in GAD

The costs of involving men in GAD or keeping men out are real — financially, practically, analytically, and even psychologically. As Catherine Scott, Asia Policy Officer of the Catholic Institute for International Relations (CIIR), stated in our interview with her:

The problem with GAD studies, in my opinion, is that they have focused exclusively on women and development and that's only half the story. In fact you could even argue that that's the less important part of it. Because to look at GAD properly, you need to look at the role of men. The role of men has been dominant and probably needs more analysis than the role of women.

Involving men in GAD entails reflecting on, and incorporating, the understanding that women are themselves integrally involved in recreating and renegotiating masculinities (Gutmann, 1997). Men, and ideas of what it means to be male, impact on women's lives, and therefore the outcome of GAD work, but the reverse is also true: women and female identities affect men and societal norms of masculinity. A number of those interviewed stressed how absurd they find the current situation in GAD work, in which women alone are expected to transform unequal gender relations. Only by enabling GAD work to focus on men and analyse masculinities can class, sexual, and ethnic differences among men be incorporated in GAD, enabling us to understand the distinction between dominant (hegemonic) ideas of what it means to be male, and more marginal alternative interpretations of masculinity.

From utilising fathering as a point of entry for involving men in GAD, to bringing men in as development workers to challenge unequal gender relations, there appears to be good evidence for supporting certain men-only efforts, provided these are established and run with leadership and control exercised by women. For this reason, among others, we are not much taken with the vogue of talking about 'new men' in GAD work: too often, this catchphrase becomes little more than a means to take a stance while avoiding the need to transform fundamental and complex — often contradictory — relations of inequality between men and women.

Ways to strengthen women in development

In her interview, Gabriela Vega of IADB underscored the importance of programmes aimed at women by pointing out: 'Unless you make women very clearly a target of your work, women can totally disappear from the framework of a project design.' She spoke of what she termed as a 'WID pipeline', which focuses on areas left out of regular development programmes, such as domestic violence, women's leadership, reproductive rights, and child-care. Christine Jones, Principal Economist in the East European Region for the World Bank, echoed these sentiments in her interview when she stated:

We need to distinguish what our objective is, which may be to improve the lives of women, versus how you go about achieving that, which may be to involve men in a way that improves the lives of women. If we start to make the improvement of men's lives a goal — moving

*beyond just involving them as a means to an end —
then all kinds of things may become confused and the
needs of women could get left by the wayside.*

Similarly, Muneera Salem-Murdock of USAID
observed in her interview:

*The reason — and this really comes from experience —
that we keep focusing on women is because experience
has really taught us that if you do not focus, if you do
not underline, if you do not specify, then more
frequently than not they tend not to be considered at all.
And you cannot do development without half the
society … When we need to focus on men in GAD, I
would welcome that time, because that means not only
have women achieved equality, but they have surpassed
it. And I would be more than happy to focus specifically
on men if they are the underclass. Absolutely. Until
that time, there's no need to focus specifically on men.*

Indeed, there is broad concern that any
attention paid to men in development work may
lead to a lessening of attention (and aid) to
women. Karen Mason, Director of Gender and
Development at the World Bank, stated in her
interview: 'I think there is still a need for WID-
type programmes, and we aren't ready to move
into a MID (Men in Development) phase.
Women are still comparatively disadvantaged.'

More broadly in the development community
of course, gender is frequently a marginalised
area of specialisation and attention that is
nonetheless allowed to exist as long as it is rather
innocuous. Andrea Murray of the British Council
implicated gender stereotypes in such toleration
of GAD when she stated: 'In a weird kind of way
you get away with gender because it's seen as soft
and fluffy even when you're being political.'
Similarly, Phil Evans of DfID noted:

*A lot of the things that we were advocating, including
women's empowerment and greater gender equality,
were seen as 'mother and apple pie', as the economists
would say. Nice stuff, sure, and we'd all like to have
them, but it's not really the front-line, nitty-gritty stuff.
It's not fundamentals.*

In other words, to employ the apt phrase of
Arturo Escobar (1995:155), a certain 'develop-
mentalisation' of women has come about, with
women, and now maybe even men, as new client
categories in development work. At a more grassroots level, there is no doubt that many women
are tired of 'doing it all' with respect to gender
inequalities. To reiterate the point made in the
Oxfam GB publication on men and masculinities:

*Focusing on women alone simply contributes to
overload and exhaustion for women, if they retain all*

*the responsibilities associated with their existing
reproductive and productive roles, in an era where the
state can be relied upon even less than previously to
provide social services* (Sweetman, 1997:2).

At the same time, there is ample reason to
continue and extend female-only programmes
and projects. Chris Roche of Oxfam UK
explained:

*A lot of the best work I think we've done in West Africa
is ensuring separate discussion with men and women,
strengthening particularly the ability of the women to
then articulate a position to men, and then involving
men in the debate.*

Clearly, women-only in practice is still widely
and profoundly, if not uniformly, necessary.

Gender and development: words and deeds

As mentioned in Chapter 5, part of the
motivation for this report comes from demands
by women involved in development projects
throughout the world. The key to involving
men in development in a way that contributes to
lessening gender and other inequalities in the
world will be a sophisticated approach to
understanding gender as relational — in other
words, recognising that gender is not simply a
matter of adding men to women, and that
involving men in development work is not
fundamentally a matter of men getting their
'fair share', men catching up with women, or
other forms of male 'me-tooism'.

With this vision, it is clear that a certain
reassertion of feminist rationales and
approaches is needed to put the inclusion of
men in development work on the best footing.
Debbie Rogow, independent consultant,
discussed in her interview the ReproSalud
programme in Peru:

*What the ReproSalud programme does is training with
men to figure out what's not working in their own lives.
And the pieces of that which dovetail with women's
needs is where change happens. It's something that in
some ways men are forced into. I mean women are
getting jobs, and these guys just have to come around
and change.*

In other words, involvement of men-as-men in
GAD should be couched within a clear feminist
political agenda. As Sarah White (1997:20-21)
writes:

*While gender-oriented programmes broadly aim to make
women less poor, as well as 'more empowered', they still*

43

tend to focus on gender in isolation from other social relations. Considering masculinity, however, points up how gender also plays a part in the other relations of inequality which structure society …Widening the picture to include consideration of men and masculinities should not simply 'count men in', but also broaden and deepen our understanding of power and inequality.

It is crucial to use the needs and priorities of women in particular local contexts to ensure that GAD policy and practice is founded on women's intimate experience with, and insights into, gender relations in specific locations. These locally-defined needs and priorities are also essential if men are to be involved in transforming gender and other relations which are built on inequality. Ann Leonard of the Population Council in New York counselled in her interview:

Always understand that things will differ from one place to another. You can't just develop a wonderful model that you then cookie cut. And since you're doing this [report] for the World Bank, which tends to do that kind of thing — if it works here, let's make 500 of them — you need to avoid that. The Bank's style is to give support to the Ministry of Health, where a lot of it never reaches the community it was intended for. In my 20 years in the field, I'd say that most of the good work that has been done has been done with really small grants.

Alongside GAD work which is grounded in specific local realities, at the same time, efforts to involve men in gender and development must draw together specialists around the world in conferences, research, and the sharing of programme and project experiences. This is parallel to the way in which 'feminist advocacy efforts have become increasingly trans-nationalised in recent years' (Alvarez, 1998:310).

Ways forward: some practical suggestions

Gender training

In considering how best to involve men in GAD, obvious questions arise around gender training. Experience exists of drawing men together in workshops to discuss gender-based inequality in relation to other forms of inequality, such as ethnicity and racism, and this is thought to have a beneficial impact. Drawing on the personal lives, experiences, and desires of men, training must help them to distinguish between a verbal recognition of the issues involved in gender

relations, and the practical changes that are needed to transform these inequalities. Such discussion must necessarily draw men into examination and debate regarding male subjectivity and psychosocial matters of emotions and authority, both in relation to women and also to other men perhaps viewed as 'less masculine'. In the field of reproductive health, for example, interventions which seek to prevent disease and unwanted pregnancy awareness must include concern for partners' health in sexuality, pregnancy, birth spacing, and childbirth.

In the same way, counselling for men and families is important for many of the complicated reasons described by Judith Helzner of the IPPF New York:

There are women who know that they need to interact or negotiate differently with their partner. Sometimes they try to abdicate responsibility and say to the health provider, 'Oh, you deal with him!' So there is a distinction between the health agency taking up the issue of dealing with men, and the health agency helping women learn how to deal with their partners. We're working on that distinction, too.

Research

Further scholarly investigation is sorely needed in the general area of men and masculinities. For example, contradictions between men's actual lives and the public stereotypes about men as fathers and husbands need to be the subject of investigations that are grounded in local meanings and practices. Such investigations are crucial in order for us to understand the diversity of experiences among men in relation to questions of sexuality, class, ethnicity, and generation. Mixed qualitative and quantitative research is needed to combine the richness of ethnographic discovery with the broader generalisations which can come from statistical data surveys on questions of reproductive health, violence, and education, to name only a few topics.[2]

For example, drawing on extensive work in developing a domestic-violence prevention programme in Nicaragua, Montoya (1998) raises the need for further comparative analysis regarding men who are violent and those who are not, as part of a broader examination of relations between men and women in couples, and of the diversity of masculine identities and practices in that country.

With respect to development agencies themselves, there is some indication that limited numbers of men are being involved in GAD work in creative ways. There are also gender issues including recruitment, training, and promotion of men, which are linked to the overall perceptions and internal priorities of their organisations in relation to GAD work. Questions of paternity leave and support to male carers are also not simply issues for the recipients of development funds, but matters to be addressed internally in development organisations.

International advocacy

The effort to promote feminist ideas and practices related to men and masculinity, regarding responsible fatherhood, for instance, is emerging as a focus of some development projects. Another area for attention is that addressed by Shepard (1996:14), when she states that at the programme level in GAD work:

If men are not educated to recognise the key role of homophobia and misogyny in their own socialisation, they will not have the intellectual or emotional resources to confront the social pressures that will inevitably besiege them as they begin to abandon traditional male sexual patterns.

Education

Pedagogical issues which related to boys regarding questions of gender, families, and children also require serious attention in development work. As Otoo-Oyortey of IPPF in London noted in our interview with her:

I mean the priority areas are really this whole area of youth. Looking at the extent to which IPPF should look at the needs of young women and young men who are using these services, relationship training for young people and bringing young people on board.

In keeping with our understanding of gender as a relational question pertaining to societies and cultures far more than biological factors, the focus on involving men in gender and development should also undoubtedly not be left simply to individual men, but must address institutional practices associated with specific male gender norms in particular historical and cultural contexts.

Concluding comments

It is taken for granted today that we must talk about women as heterogeneous rather than homogeneous in gender and development, taking into account the tremendous diversity of experiences and beliefs of women in different countries and cultures throughout the world. The same is less true with respect to distinctions between men: it is still common to find sweeping generalisations about the males of the species, as if, ironically enough, being a man made one 'naturally' think and act in certain ways.

We have tried in this report to underline the complexity of matters related to men. For example, we have noted that there is diversity among men, and there are different masculinities. We have noted, too, that men are gendered human beings, and themselves reinforce or resist dominant forms of masculinity, both as individuals and in influencing, socialising, and educating others. Noting these things is not to deny the broad patterns of gender inequalities between women and men in particular cultural contexts, and in the world as a whole. Rather, identifying these things is the only possible means by which development researchers, policy-makers, and practitioners can understand and transform unequal gender relations. Only by considering men in this way can we (to quote Sree Gururaja of UNICEF in her interview) ' ... make men part of the solution, rather than part of the problem'.

As our interviews made clear, the demand that men be incorporated in an increasing number and range of GAD projects has often originated from women at the grassroots. Further, as became clear in our interviews, the involvement of men in one aspect of development work — for example, in work to end domestic violence — inevitably has repercussions for other issues, such as fatherhood and reproductive rights. In these and other ways, development workers can utilise a variety of development models based on perceived local conditions and requirements (and far less on the exigencies of centralised agencies and institutions). If this occurs, we can, as suggested in Chapter 1, best address 'the desirability, potential, and prospects for a more male-inclusive approach to gender and development'.

45

Appendix 1: Interview guide for organisations

Preliminary background details

When was your organisation founded?

What were the aims and remit when it was first founded? And how have these changed over the years?

What do you feel are your remit and responsibilities in the late 1990s?

How many staff do you have in total (including volunteers)? How does staff composition break down by grade/position? And how do these grades themselves break down by gender?

What kind of budget does your organisation control?

General

What is your organisation's understanding of 'gender' in the gender and development field?

How has gender informed policy and intervention strategies within your organisation?

What have been the explicit aims of this approach?

Have these aims been achieved in your view? If not, why?

Has your organisation worked with any particular kind of gender-planning framework (e.g. Harvard, Moser, Social Relations, Women's Empowerment, Longwe)?

Do you feel that understandings of, and approaches to, gender have changed over time, and at which operational levels in your organisation? In which ways? And which areas of activity? Why?

Does your organisation make an internal differentiation of gender, of different groups of men and women? Which particular groups of men and women are the focus of different interventions?

How does this translate into a development policy context? More specifically, how do you approach questions of gendered analysis in terms of development while attending to a differentiated understanding of gender?

What role do you think that gender should take within development organisations (i.e. what remit should development organisations have — gender blind, gender neutral, gender specific, etc.)?

Men in GAD

How do you understand the position of men within the concept of gender? Do you think that men are, or should, be considered as a gender within GAD perspectives?

How do you think this relates to current perspectives within GAD?

What do you think are the implications of omitting men from GAD interventions?

And what do you perceive to be the implications of including them?

More specifically, how does your organisation approach 'men' both in a policy and project context?

Has your organisation led on any initiatives that have focused on men, or groups of men, and if so what has been the rationale behind this? What criteria/strategy was used to determine the group to be targeted for development assistance, and what are the wider implications of this for the rest of your work in the development field?

Referring back to internal differentiation, what merits and demerits do you feel there are in thinking through 'men' as a heterogeneous group?

What implications does this have for the way in which you look at questions of power, access and resources, and the practical context of project design, for instance?

Men, GAD, and the political environment of development organisations

How are gendered policies formulated and operationalised through your organisation? For example, is there a separate department overseeing dimensions of gender within development work, is it an integrated part of all levels of development organisations, or a combination of both?

And how do issues relating to gender inform the internal composition of staff? What proportion of staff is male and female at different levels of the organisation, and what training on gender issues do these staff receive? What forms of project worker and policy-specific gender training are there?

And how does that relate to conceptualising men within GAD? Does your staff training and composition reflect a move from WID to GAD?

If not already present how do you think that training on men in GAD, particularly project staff, would be welcomed or resisted within your organisation, and why?

What do you feel are the implications of having, or not having, men themselves
- within the policy department of your organisation?
- at an operational level as project workers?

GAD in the new millennium

How do you see your work progressing in the next millennium?

What will be the key priority areas?

What changes would you like to see in a GAD context and what changes in policy and practice are your organisation planning, or hoping, to implement?

How do you feel gender will frame these endeavours, and will men be located within this?

Appendix 2: Individuals and organisations consulted

Abantu for Development
Rabiya Balwea
1 Winchester House
11 Cranmer Road
London SW9
UK

ActionAid
Kate Metcalf and Bimal
    Phnuyal
International Education
    Unit
Hamlyn House
Macdonald Rd
Archway London
N19 5PG
UK

AVSC International
Eliza Mahoney
79 Madison Ave
New York
NY 10016
USA

British Council
Andrea Murray
Gender Consultant
Head of Gender Team
Bridgewater House
58 Witworth St.
Manchester
M1 6BB
UK

**Catholic Fund for
Overseas Development
(CAFOD)**
Elizabeth Wade-Brown
Evaluation Officer
Romero Close
Stockwell Rd
London
SW9 9TY
UK

**Catholic Institute for
International Relations
(CIIR)**
Catherine Scott
Asia Policy Officer
Unit 3
Canonbury Yard
190a New North Road
London
N1 7BJ
UK

**Commonwealth
Foundation**
Sharon Robinson
Marlboro House
Pall Mall
London
SW1Y 5HX
UK

**Commonwealth
Secretariat**
Rawida Baksh-Soodeen
Chief Programme Officer
GYAD
5th Floor
55 Pall Mall
London
SW1Y 5HX
UK

**Commonwealth
Secretariat**
Nancy Spence
Head of GAD
5th Floor
55 Pall Mall
London
SW1Y 5HX
UK

**Department for
International
Development (DfID)**
Phil Evans
Social Development
    Division
94 Victoria St.
London
SW1E 5JL
UK

Independent Consultant
Debbie Rogow
709 W. Mt. Airy Ave
Philadelphia
PA 19119
USA

**Inter-American
Development Bank
(IADB)**
Gabriela Vega
Social Development
    Specialist
1300 New York Ave NW
Washington
DC 20577
USA

**Interaction-Commission
on the Advancement of
Women**
Suzanne Kindervatter
Director
Suite 701
1717 Massachussetts Ave
    NW
Washington
DC 20036
USA

**International Monetary
Fund (IMF)**
Ratna Sahay
Research Department
700 19th St NW
Washington
DC 20431
USA

**International Planned
Parenthood Federation
Western Hemisphere
Region (IPPF/WHR)**
Judith Helzner
Director of Sexual and
    Reproductive Health
120 Wall St
9th Floor
New York
NY 10005-3902
USA

**International Planned
Parenthood Federation
(IPPF)**
Naana Otoo-Oyortey
Inner Circle
Regents Park
London
NW1 4NS
UK

**Office of Women in
Development, United
States Agency for
International
Development (USAID)**
Muneera Salem-Murdock
Deputy Director
Ronald Reagan Building
1300 Pennsylvania Ave
    NW
Washington
DC 20523
USA

One World Action
Helen O'Connell
Education and Policy
    Co-ordinator
Bradleys Close
White Lion St
London N1 3PF
UK

**Overseas Development
Institute (ODI)**
Simon Maxwell
Director
Portland House
Stag Place
London
SW1E 5DP
UK

Oxfam GB
Chris Roche
Head of Programme
Policy Team
Oxfam House
274 Banbury Road
OX2 7DZ
UK

Population Council
Wesley Clark
1 Dag Hammarskjöld
    Plaza
9th Floor
New York
NY 10017
USA

Population Council
Ann Leonard
Program Associate
1 Dag Hammarskjöld
    Plaza
9th Floor
New York
NY 10017
USA

Salud y Género
Benno de Keijzer
Margarita Maza de Juarez
    No. 13
Colonia Unidad Jardin
Xalapa Veracruz 91170
México

**United Nations
Children's Fund
(UNICEF)**
Sree Gururaja
333 East 28th St
New York
NY 10016
USA

**United Nations
Development Fund for
Women (UNIFEM)
Bangkok**
Dr Lorraine Corner
Head of UNIFEM
    Bangkok
c/o UNDP UN Bldg.
Bajdamnern Nok Ave
Bangkok 10200
Thailand

**United Nations
Development
Programme (UNDP),
Gender in Development
Programme (GIDP)**
James Lang
Rm 2040
20th Fl., DC1
1 UN Plaza
New York
NY 10017
USA

**United Nations
Development
Programme (UNDP),
Gender in Development
Programme (GIDP)**
Cecil Taffe
Rm 2040
20th Fl., DC1
1 UN Plaza
New York
NY 10017
USA

**United Nations
Development
Programme (UNDP),
Gender in Development
Programme (GIDP)**
Ove Bjerregaard
Rm 2040
20th Fl., DC1
1 UN Plaza
New York
NY 10017
USA

**Women in Development
(WID) Strat Project,
Office of Women in
Development, USAID**
Deborah Caro
Project Director
Suite 810
1000 16th St NW
Washington
DC 20036
USA

**Women in Development
(WID) Strat Project,
Office of Women in
Development, USAID**
Deborah Rubin
Economic Growth
    Advisor
Suite 810
1000 16th St NW
Washington
DC 20036
USA

Womankind Worldwide
Helen Pankhurst
Head of International
    Programmes
The Hub
3 Albion Place
Galena Rd
Hammersmith
London
W6 OLT
UK

World Bank
Christine Jones
Principal Economist
East European Region
World Bank
1818 H. St NW
Washington
DC 20433
USA

World Bank
Karen Mason
Director
Gender and Development
World Bank
1818 H. St NW
Washington
DC 20433
USA

World Bank
Shimwaayi Muntemba
Social Scientist
World Bank
1818 H. St NW
Washington
DC 20433
USA

World Bank
Vijayendra Rao
Economist
World Bank
1818 H. St NW
Washington
DC 20433
USA

World Bank
Susan Razzaz
Gender Specialist
World Bank
1818 H. St NW
Washington
DC 20433
USA

World Bank
Shaha Riza
Gender Specialist
World Bank
1818 H. St NW
Washington
DC 20433
USA

Notes

Chapter 1

1. This sub-title is an adaptation of the title of a paper 'Which Men, Why Now?' given by Ruth Pearson at the second of five conferences in a seminar series on 'Men, Masculinities and Gender Relations in Development' funded by the Economic and Social Research Council (ESRC), UK, between 1998 and 2000 (see Pearson, 1999). We are grateful to Professor Pearson for giving us permission to use this adaptation.

2. Although there are elaborate (and contested) typologies of *'de jure'* and *'de facto'* female household headship, the term *de jure* woman-headed household usually refers to a unit in which women live without a male partner on a more or less permanent basis and receive no economic support from one, except in the form of legally-prescribed child maintenance (which is low and poorly-enforced in most developing countries). *De facto* female-headed households, alternatively, either denote households that are temporarily headed by women (due to male labour migration), or ones in which women play the primary role in the economic support of dependent members (see Chant, 1997a:15-18).

3. As an example, in the first four conferences held under the auspices of the ESRC seminar series detailed in Note 1 (in Bradford, September 1998, Norwich, June and September 1999, and London, January 2000, respectively), women have greatly out-numbered men on both occasions.

Chapter 2

1. The 'feminisation of poverty' became something of a new orthodoxy in gender and development in the 1990s. Although often rather casually defined, it is widely identified as a global phenomenon, and is generally understood as referring to the increased *numbers* of women in poverty, and to increased *degrees* of poverty among women. It is also frequently associated with the worldwide rise in proportions of households headed by women, even if the empirical evidence for a systematic relationship between the 'feminisation of poverty' and 'feminisation of household headship' appears somewhat tenuous (see Chant, 1997a: Chapter 2).

2. Empowerment as conceived by women in the South may be very different to Empowerment as understood by development agencies, however. Kate Young (1993) notes that the latter have tended to translate this as 'entrepreneurial self-reliance'.

3. This applies *within* as much as *between* institutions. For example, Moser *et al.*'s (1999) study on mainstreaming in the World Bank documents wide differences in rationales, language, and underlying policy approach to GAD within the Bank itself, as well as highlighting considerable diversity of formal policy statements about GAD among selected international agencies (ibid.:12).

4. In the light of this statement, it may appear paradoxical that the staffing breakdown within the Norwegian Agency for Development Cooperation (NORAD) continues to show a decidedly uneven gender distribution. Although there was greater movement of women into male-dominated tiers of the employment hierarchy between 1985 and 1992 (during which time the overall proportion of women employed in the organisation actually declined from 63.6 per cent to 59.3 per cent), this was mainly at intermediate levels (senior/special advisors and senior executive officers) rather than upper levels (directors and heads of division). Moreover, at the bottom of the scale (junior executive officers and clerks/messengers), over 80 per cent of employees were women (Jahan, 1995:131).

5. In brief, Caroline Moser's Triple Roles framework aims to raise gender awareness in planning by pointing out how women have three major roles (reproduction,

production, and community management) and that their capacity to participate in planned interventions will be affected by their involvement in these three domains (see Moser, 1989, 1993). The main focus of the Triple Roles framework has been low-income households, and one of the principal thrusts of Moser's work has been to emphasise that lack of recognition of women's unpaid work in their homes and communities by men and by planners has led to policies that exploit women, often intensify gender inequalities, and give women little in the way of power or resources to challenge their subordinate position. A more recent alternative to Moser's framework is presented by Naila Kabeer's Social Relations framework. This pays greater attention to the interaction of gender with other forms of social inequality such as class, race, and religion, and extends beyond the sphere of the household to encompass other sites of power. Under a social relations perspective, Kabeer (1994a:281) asserts that: 'Gender awareness in policy and planning requires a prior analysis of the social relations of production within relevant institutions of family, market, state, and community in order to understand how gender and other inequalities are created and reproduced though their separate and combined interactions.'

6. While Naila Kabeer (1994a,b) in her Social Relations framework for gender planning talks about 'practical gender-based needs', she retains Molyneux's original term 'interests' when referring to strategic gender interests. Kabeer's reasons for so-doing revolve around the fact that Molyneux's work was grounded within a Marxist theoretical tradition where interests arise out of power relations and are defined differently according to people's positions in the social and economic order. For disadvantaged groups, therefore, the identification of strategic interests can only really emerge 'from below'. The term 'needs', alternatively, belongs to planning discourse, and given the social constitution of organisations, is 'generally a perspective from above' (Kabeer, 1994a:297).

Kabeer further notes that 'the distinction between needs and interests would be a purely semantic one if all planning processes were transparent, participatory,

democratic and accountable'. This is rarely the case, however. Institutions are sites of contested power relations between different groups, where men's strategic gender interests (which might include protecting their position or extending their privileges) may clearly present obstacles to the pursuit and/or attainment of women's strategic gender interests (see also Goetz, 1995; White, 1994).

Jo Beall (1995b) also adheres to the practical needs/strategic interests schema, further clarifying the importance of terminological differences by identifying that interests are held by political or organisational categories of people i.e. interest groups who advance their *demands*, whereas needs are identified *for* beneficiaries or *by* users within the planning process, whether in a 'top-down' or 'bottom-up' way. Unlike Moser, therefore, Beall does not regard political/organisational and political/planning processes as interchangeable. This aside, the utility of working with an interests perspective is that in the context of 'process' projects (i.e. participatory projects in which, alongside practical components such as water and housing, there is some provision for capacity-building, consciousness-raising and so on), this allows different actors (for example, planners, beneficiaries and so on) to go as far as they are able/willing to go and thus gives greater flexibility.

Chapter 3

1. 'Gender-neutral' policy is a term coined by Naila Kabeer (1994b:81-4) as part of a three-fold categorisation of gender policies as follows:

(i) *gender-neutral policies* — 'top-down' policies, which are not concerned with changing gender divisions of resources or responsibilities, but need reliable information about gender in order to target the actors who will facilitate the most efficient realisation of policy goals;

(ii) *gender-specific policies* — policies that are concerned with women, and direct activities and resources to women as a means of strengthening their position. The mere fact of targeting women only, however, is unlikely to provoke major changes in gender roles or relations, although it would be interesting in evaluations to explore the extent to which changes arise, especially as Kabeer (1994b:82) points out that different approaches 'need not cancel each other out';

(iii) *gender-redistributive/transformative policies* — policies that have the explicit objective of redistributing resources, responsibilities and power between men and women. This is clearly the most challenging alternative since 'it does not simply seek to channel resources to women within the existing framework, but may require men to give up certain privileges and take on certain responsibilities in order to achieve greater equity in development outcomes' (Kabeer, 1994b:82). While these might be difficult to introduce, they could conceivably emerge out of other types of intervention and in the final analysis begin to address strategic gender interests.

2. Foreman (1999:20), for example, notes that among male political and religious leaders, fear of losing authority can lead to active attempts to block educational and economic advances for women.

3. This statement, cited in Kabeer (1994a:1), was made by a delegate at the 1991 Women's Studies Conference in London.

Chapter 5

1. See Lerner (1998) for a pioneering collection of studies on this question. For case studies from Peru and Colombia, see Cáceres (1998) and Viveros (1998) respectively.

2. The argument in Herdt (1994) and elsewhere is emphatically that sexuality is not dichotomous; that is, that there are more than neatly categorisable 'male' and 'female' sexualities in the world and that sexuality is more than the simple social expression of processes governed by one's biological genitalia.

3. Personal communication, Teresita de Barbieri, Instituto de Investigaciones Sociales, Universidad Nacional Autónoma de México, January 1999.

4. It will come as no surprise that the vast majority of individuals we consulted for this report were women (see Appendix 2).

5. We are grateful to Ramya Subrahmanian of the Institute of Development Studies, Sussex, UK, for her insights here. See also Farnsveden and Rönquist (1999:3).

Chapter 6

1. See Teresita de Barbieri (1992) for an excellent discussion of the notion of patriarchy in Latin America.

2. Yet, as Corner (1996:69, 74n) notes: 'Quantitative methods are particularly destructive to the interests of women because they are heavily dependent on data, from which women tend to be excluded.' If this is true with respect to women in areas such as applied economics, it is probably also true with respect to men in certain areas such as housework and childcare.

References

ActionAid (1998) *Institutionalising Gender in ActionAid*, ActionAid: London.

Alvarez, Sonia (1998) 'Latin American feminisms "go global": trends of the 1990s and challenges for the new millennium', in Sonia E. Alvarez, Evelina Dagnino, and Arturo Escobar (eds), *Cultures of Politics/Politics of Cultures: Revisioning Latin American Social Movements*, Westview: Boulder, 293–324.

Andersen, Cecilia (1992) 'Practical guidelines', in Lise Østergaard (ed.), *Gender and Development*, Routledge: London, 165–97.

Armstrong, Bruce, Alwyn T. Cohall, Roger D. Vaughan, McColvin Scott, Lorraine Tiezzi, and James F. McCarthy (1999) 'Involving men in reproductive health: The Young Men's Clinic', *American Journal of Public Health*, 89:6, 902–05.

Barker, Gary (1997) 'Emerging Global Trends Related to the Role of Men and Families', briefing notes for a Brown Bag Discussion organised by the Chapin Hall Center for Children at the University of Chicago, October.

Beall, Jo (1995a) 'In sickness and in health: engendering health policy for development', *Third World Planning Review*, 17:2, 213–22.

Beall, Jo (1995b) 'Gender, Development and Social Planning' (SA412), MSc course outline, Department of Social Policy, London School of Economics, London.

Bhasin, Kamla (1997) 'Gender workshops with men: experiences and reflections', *Gender and Development*, Oxfam, 5:2, 55–61.

Blumberg, Rae Lesser (1995) 'Introduction: Engendering wealth and well-being in an era of economic transformation', in Rae Lesser Blumberg, Cathy Rakowski, Irene Tinker, and Michael Monteón (eds), *Engendering Wealth and Well-Being: Empowerment for Global Change*, Westview: Boulder, 1–14.

Budowski, Monica and Laura Guzmán, (1998) 'Strategic Gender Interests in Social Policy: Empowerment Training for Female Heads of Household in Costa Rica', paper prepared for the International Sociological Association XIV World Congress of Sociology, Montreal, 26 July–1 August.

Buvinic, Mayra (1983) 'Women's issues in Third World poverty: a policy analysis', in Marya Buvinic, Margaret Lycette, and William McGreevy (eds), *Women and Poverty in the Third World*, John Hopkins University Press: Baltimore, 13–34.

Buvinic, Mayra (1985) 'Projects for women in the Third World: explaining their "misbehaviour"', *World Development*, 14:5, 653–64.

Cáceres, Carlos (1998) 'Jóvenes varones en Lima: dilemas y estrategias en salud sexual' in Teresa Valdés and José Olavarría (eds), *Masculinidades y equidad de género en América Latina*, FLACSO/UNFPA: Santiago, Chile, 158–74.

Campbell, Cathy (1997a) 'Migrancy, masculine identities and AIDS: the psychosocial context of HIV transmission on the South African gold mines', *Social Science and Medicine*, 45:2, 273–81.

Campbell, Cathy (1997b) 'Selling Sex in the Time of AIDS: Gender, HIV and Commercial Sex Work in Southern Africa', paper delivered at the 'Masculinities in Question' Seminar Series, Gender Institute, London School of Economics, 12 November.

Castells, Manuel (1997) *The Power of Identity*, Blackwell: Oxford.

Chant, Sylvia (1985) 'Single-parent families: choice or constraint? The formation of female-headed households in Mexican shanty towns', *Development and Change*, 16:4, 635–6.

Chant, Sylvia (1995a) 'Editorial introduction: gender and development in the 1990s', *Third World Planning Review* (special issue on Gender and Development), 17:2, 111–6.

Chant, Sylvia (1995b) 'Policy approaches to women and gender in developing countries: an overview', paper prepared for the Commonwealth Secretariat, Commonwealth Youth Programme Planning Meeting, Maidstone, Kent, 8 December.

Chant, Sylvia (1997a) *Women-headed Households: Diversity and Dynamics in the Developing World*, Macmillan: Basingstoke.

Chant, Sylvia (1997b) 'Men, Households and Poverty in Costa Rica: A Pilot Study', final report to the Economic and Social Research Council, UK (Award No. R000222205).

Chant, Sylvia (1999) 'Youth, Gender and "Family Crisis" in Costa Rica', report to the Nuffield Foundation, London (Award No. SGS/LB/0223).

Chant, Sylvia (2000a) 'From "woman-blind" to "man-kind": should men have more space in gender and development?', *IDS Bulletin* (Sussex), 31:2, 7–17.

Chant, Sylvia (2000b) 'Men in crisis? Reflections on masculinities, work and family in northwest Costa Rica', *European Journal of Development Research*, 12:2.

Chant, Sylvia and Cathy McIlwaine (1995) *Women of a Lesser Cost: Female Labour, Foreign Exchange and Philippine Development*, Pluto: London.

Chant, Sylvia and Cathy McIlwaine (1998) *Three Generations, Two Genders, One World: Women and Men in a Changing Century*, Zed: London.

Chen, Marty (1989) 'A sectoral approach to promoting women's work: lessons from India', *World Development*, 17:7, 1007–16.

Commission of the European Communities (CEC) (1992) 'Women in Development', Directorate-General, EC: Brussels.

Commonwealth Secretariat (1995a) 'The 1995 Commonwealth Plan of Action on Gender and Development', Commonwealth Secretariat: London.

Commonwealth Secretariat (1995b) 'Working Towards Gender Equality', Commonwealth Secretariat: London.

Commonwealth Secretariat (1995c) 'Working towards gender equality : programme initiatives', Commonwealth Secretariat: London.

Connell, Robert W. (1987) *Gender and Power: Society, the Person and Sexual Politics*, Stanford University Press: Stanford.

Corner, Lorraine (1996) *Women, Men and Economics: The Gender-Differentiated Impacts of Macroeconomics*, UNIFEM: New York.

Cornwall, Andrea (1997) 'Men, masculinity and "gender in development"', in Caroline Sweetman (ed.), *Men and Masculinity*, Oxfam: Oxford, 8–13.

Cornwall, Andrea (1998) 'Gender, participation and the politics of difference', in Irene Guijt and Meera Kaul Shah (eds), *The Myth of Community: Gender Issues in Participatory Development*, Intermediate Technology Publications: London, 46–57.

Dawson, Elsa (1995) 'Women, Gender and Impact Assessment: A Discussion Paper', presented at the Development Studies Association Conference, Dublin, 7–9 September.

de Keijzer, Benno (1998) 'El varón como factor de riesgo', in *Familias y Relaciones de Género en Transformación: Cambios Transcendentales en América Latina*, Population Council/EDAMEX: Mexico City.

Department for International Development (DfID) (1998) 'Breaking the Barriers: Women and the Elimination of World Poverty', DfID: London.

Development Planning Unit (DPU) (1999) 'DPU Gender Policy and Planning Programme', DPU, University College London: London.

Elson, Diane (1989) 'The impact of structural adjustment on women: concepts and issues', in Bade Onimode (ed.), *The IMF, the World Bank and the African Debt. Vol. 2: The Social and Political Impact*, Zed: London, 55–74.

Elson, Diane (1991) 'Structural adjustment: its effects on women', in Tina Wallace with Candida March (eds), *Changing Perceptions: Writings on Gender and Development*, Oxfam: Oxford, 39–53.

Engle, Patrice L. (1997) 'The role of men in families: achieving gender equity and supporting children', in Caroline Sweetman (ed.), *Men and Masculinity*, Oxfam: Oxford, 31–40.

Engle, Patrice L. and Cynthia Breaux (1994) *Is there a Father Instinct? Fathers' Responsibility for Children*, Population Council/International Center for Research on Women: New York/Washington DC.

Engle, Patrice L. and Javier Alatorre Rico (1994) *Taller Sobre Paternidad Responsable*, Population Council/International Center for Research on Women: New York/Washington DC).

Escobar, Arturo (1995) *Encountering Development: The Making and Unmaking of the Third World*, Princeton University Press: Princeton, NJ.

Escobar Latapí, Agustin (1998) 'Los hombres y sus historias: reestructuración y masculinidad en México', *La Ventana*, Universidad de Guadalajara, 5:122–173.

Färnsveden, Ulf and Anders Rönquist (1999) 'Why Men? A Pilot Study of the Existing Attitudes among SIDA's Staff towards Male Participation in the Promotion of Gender Equality in Development', unpublished Masters dissertation, Peace and Development Research Institute, Göteborg University.

Fernando, Marina (1985) 'New skills for women: a community development project in Colombo, Sri Lanka', in Caroline Moser and Linda Peake (eds), *Women, Human Settlements and Housing*, Tavistock: London, 88–112.

Figueroa Perea, Juan Guillermo (1998) 'Algunos elementos para interpretar la presencia de los varones en los procesos de salud reproductiva', *Revista de Cadernos de Saúde Pública*, Brazil, Vol. 14, supplemento 1, 87–96.

Folbre, Nancy (1994) *Who Pays for the Kids? Gender and Structures of Constraint*, Routledge: London.

Fonseca, Claudia (1991) 'Spouses, siblings and sex-linked bonding : a look at kinship organization in a Brazilian slum', in Elizabeth Jelin (ed.), *Family, Household and Gender Relations in Latin America*, Kegan Paul International, UNESCO: New York, 133–160.

Foreman, Martin (1999) *AIDS and Men: Taking Risks or Taking Responsibility*, Panos Institute: London.

Goetz, Anne Marie (1995) 'Institutionalising women's interests and accountability to women in development', *IDS Bulletin* (Sussex), 26:3, 1–10.

Goetz, Anne Marie (1997) 'Introduction' , in Anne Marie Goetz (ed.), *Getting Institutions Right for Women in Development*, Zed: London, 1–28.

Goetz, Anne Marie and Reeta Sen Gupta (1996) 'Who takes the credit? Gender, power and control over loan use in rural credit programmes in Bangladesh', *World Development*, 24:1, 45–63.

Gomáriz, Enrique (1997) 'Introducción a los Estudios Sobre la Masculinidad', Centro Nacional para el Desarrollo de la Mujer y Familia: San José.

González de la Rocha, Mercedes (ed.) (1999) *Divergencias del Modelo Tradicional: Hogares de Jefatura Femenina en América Latina*, Centro de Investigaciones y Estudios Superiores en Antropología Social: México DF.

Goodwin, Rick (1997) 'The Other Half of the Sky: Focused Work on Men and Gender Justice in Tamil Nadu, India', mimeo, Womankind Worldwide, London.

Grown, Caren and Jennefer Sebstad (1989) 'Introduction: Towards a wider perspective on women's employment', *World Development*, 17:7, 937–52.

Güendel, Ludwig and Mauricio González (1998) 'Integration, human rights and social policy in the context of human poverty', in UNICEF (ed.), *Adolescence, Child Rights and Urban Poverty in Costa Rica*, UNICEF/HABITAT: San José, 17–31.

Gutmann, Matthew C. (1996) *The Meanings of Macho: Being a Man in Mexico City*, University of California Press: Berkeley.

Gutmann, Matthew C. (1997) 'The ethnographic (G) ambit: women and the negotiation of masculinity in Mexico City', *American Ethnologist* 24:4, 833–55.

Gutmann, Matthew C. (1998) 'Mamitis and the traumas of development in a *colonia popular* of Mexico City', in Nancy Scheper-Hughes and Carolyn Sargent (eds), *Small Wars: The Cultural Politics of Childhood*, University of California Press: Berkeley, 130–48.

Hardon, Anita and Elizabeth Hayes (eds) (1997) *Reproductive Rights in Practice: A Feminist Report on the Quality of Care*, Zed: London.

Harrison, Elizabeth (1997a) 'Men in women's groups: interlopers or allies?', *IDS Bulletin*, 28:3, 122–32.

Harrison, Elizabeth (1997b) 'Fish, feminists and the FAO: translating "gender" through different institutions in the development process', in Anne Marie Goetz (ed.), *Getting Institutions Right for Women in Development*, Zed: London, 61–74.

Harvey, David (1989) *The Condition of Postmodernity: An Enquiry into the Origins of Cultural Change*, Cambridge, MA: Blackwell.

Hearn, Jeff (1998) 'Troubled masculinities in social policy discourses: young men', in Jennie Popay, Jeff Hearn, and Jeanette Edwards (eds), *Men, Gender Divisions and Welfare*, Routledge: London, 37–62.

Helzner, Judith (1996a) 'Gender equality remains the objective', in *International Planned Parenthood Federation Challenges: Men's Needs and Responsibilities*, IPPF: London, 4–7.

Helzner, Judith F. (1996b) 'Men's involvement in family planning', *Reproductive Health Matters*, 7:146–54.

Herdt, Gilbert (1994) *Third Sex, Third Gender: Beyond Sexual Dimorphism in Culture and History*, Zone Books: New York.

Humble, Morag (1998) 'Assessing PRA for implementing gender and development', in Irene Guijt and Meera Kaul Shah (eds), *The Myth of Community: Gender Issues in Participatory Development*, Intermediate Technology Publications: London, 35–45.

IDS Bulletin (Sussex) 26:3 (1995) 'Getting Institutions Right for Women in Development'.

Instituto Mixto de Ayuda Social (IMAS) (1999) 'Programa Construyendo Oportunidades', IMAS: San José.

International Planned Parenthood Federation (IPPF) (1993) 'Strategic Plan: Vision 2000', IPPF: London.

International Planned Parenthood Federation (IPPF) (1996a) 'Challenges: Men's Needs and Responsibilities', IPPF: London.

International Planned Parenthood Federation (IPPF) (1996b) Africa Link: 'Just for Men: Involving Men in Sexual and Reproductive Health Programmes', IPPF: London.

International Planned Parenthood Federation (IPPF) (1998) *IPPF Handbook on Gender Equity and Reproductive Health*, IPPF: London.

Jackson, Cecile (1999) 'Men's work, masculinities and gender divisions of labour', *Journal of Development Studies*, 36:1, 89–108.

Jahan, Rounaq (1995) *The Elusive Agenda: Mainstreaming Women in Development*, Zed:London.

Jiménez, Rodrigo (1996) 'Adios al patriarca', in ILANUD, *Construcción de la Identidad Masculina*, Instituto Latinamericano de Naciones Unidas para la Prevención y Tratamiento del Delincuente: San José, 43–6.

Johnstone, Sarah (1999) 'Draft Gender Policy', mimeo, Womankind Worldwide: London.

Kabeer, Naila (1994a) *Reversed Realities: Gender Hierarchies in Development Thought*, Verso: London.

Kabeer, Naila (1994b) 'Gender-aware policy and planning: a social relations perspective', in Mandy MacDonald (ed.), *Gender Planning in Development Agencies: Meeting the Challenge*, Oxfam: Oxford, 80–97.

Kabeer, Naila (1998) '"Money Can't Buy Me Love?": Re-evaluating Gender, Credit and Empowerment in Rural Bangladesh', IDS Discussion Paper No. 363, Institute of Development Studies, Sussex: Brighton.

Kabeer, Naila and Ramya Subrahmanian (1996) 'Institutions, relations and outcomes: framework and tools for gender-aware planning', Discussion Paper No. 357, Institute of Development Studies, Sussex: Brighton.

Kajifusa, Hiroki (1998) 'Towards Mainstreaming Gender Issues in Development Institutions: The Possibilities and Limitations of Men's Involvement in WID/GAD', unpublished MSc dissertation, Institute of Development Studies, University of Sussex, Brighton.

Kanji, Nazneen (1995): 'ODA Gender Planning Workshops in Kenya', briefing document, Overseas Development Administration: London.

Karl, Marilee (1995) *Women and Empowerment: Participation and Decision-making*, Zed: London.

Kaztman, Rubén (1992) 'Por qué los hombres son tan irresponsables?', *Revista de la CEPAL*, 46, 1–9.

Large, Judith (1997) 'Disintegration conflicts and the restructuring of masculinity', in Caroline Sweetman (ed.), *Men and Masculinity*, Oxfam: Oxford, 23–30.

Lerner, Susana (ed.) (1998) *Varones, Sexualidad y Reproducción*, El Colegio de México: Mexico City.

Levy, Caren (1992) 'Gender and the environment: the challenge of cross-cutting issues' in *Development Policy and Planning, Environment and Urbanisation*, 4:1, 134–49.

Levy, Caren (1996) 'The Process of Institutionalising Gender in Policy and Planning: The "Web" of Institutionalisation', Working Paper No.74, Development Planning Unit, University College London: London.

Levy, Caren (1998) 'Institutionalisation of gender through participatory practice', in Irene Guijt and Meera Kaul Shah (eds), *The Myth of Community: Gender Issues in Participatory Development*, Intermediate Technology Publications: London, 254–67.

Levy, Caren (1999) 'The Relationships between Policy Approaches to Development and to Women and Gender International Agency Policies', training handout, DPU Gender Policy and Planning Programme, Development Planning Unit, University College London.

Longwe, Sara Hlupekile (1991) 'Gender awareness: the missing element in the Third World development project', in Tina Wallace with Candida March (eds) *Changing Perceptions: Writings on Gender and Development*, Oxfam: Oxford,149–57.

Longwe, Sara Hlupekile (1995) 'A development agency as a patriarchal cooking pot: the evaporation of policies for women's advancement', in Mandy MacDonald (compiler), *Women's Rights and Development*, Working Paper, Oxfam: Oxford, 18–29.

Lotherington, Anne Therese and Anne Britt Flemmen (1991) 'Negotiating gender: the case of the International Labour Organisation (ILO)', in Kristi Anne Stølen and Mariken Vaa (eds) *Gender and Change in Developing Countries*, Norwegian University Press: Oslo, 273–307.

Lumsden, Ian (1996) *Machos, Maricones and Gays: Cuba and Homosexuality*, Temple University Press/Latin America Bureau: Philadelphia/London.

MacDonald, Mandy (ed.) (1994) *Gender Planning in Development Agencies: Meeting the Challenge*, Oxfam: Oxford.

MacDonald, Mandy (compiler) (1995) 'Women's Rights and Development', Working Paper, Oxfam: Oxford.

MacDonald, Mandy, Ellen Sprenger, and Ireen Dubel (1997) *Gender and Organisational Change: Bridging the Gap Between Policy and Practice*, Royal Tropical Institute: Amsterdam.

March, Candida, Ines Smyth, and Maitrayee Mukhopadhyay (1999) *A Guide to Gender Analysis Frameworks*, Oxfam: Oxford.

Mehta, Mona (1991) 'Analysis of a development programme', in Tina Wallace with Candida March (eds), *Changing Perceptions: Writings on Gender and Development*, Oxfam: Oxford, 141–8.

Mayoux, Linda (1991) 'The poverty of income generation: a critique of women's handicraft schemes in India', in Tina Wallace with Candida March (eds), *Changing Perceptions: Writings on Gender and Development*, Oxfam: Oxford, 219–35.

Metcalf, Kate and Geni Gomez (1998) 'Gender and Reflect, PLA Notes: Participatory Learning and Action', ActionAid: London, No.32.

Molyneux, Maxine (1984) 'Mobilisation Without Emancipation?', *Critical Social Policy 10*, 4:7, 59–75.

Molyneux, Maxine (1986) 'Mobilisation without emancipation? Women's interests, state and revolution in Nicaragua', in Richard Fagan, Carmen Diana Deere, and José Luís Coraggio (eds), *Transition and Development: Problems of Third World Socialism*, Monthly Review Press: New York, 280–302.

Montoya Tellería, Oswaldo (1998) *Nadando Contra Corriente: Buscando Pistas para Prevenir la Violencia Masculina en las Relaciones de Pareja*, Puntos de Encuentro: Managua.

Moore, Henrietta (1994) 'Is There a Crisis in the Family?', Occasional Paper 3, World Summit for Social Development. UNRISD: Geneva.

Moser, Caroline (1987) 'Women, human settlements and housing: a conceptual framework for analysis and policy-Making', in Caroline Moser and Linda Peake (eds), *Women, Human Settlements and Housing*, Tavistock: London, 12–32.

Moser, Caroline (1989) 'Gender planning in the Third World: meeting practical and strategic gender needs', *World Development*,17:11, 1799–1825.

Moser, Caroline (1993) *Gender Planning and Development*, Routledge: London.

Moser, Caroline and Caren Levy (1986) 'A Theory and Methodology of Gender Planning: Meeting Women's Practical and Strategic Gender Needs', Gender and Planning Working Paper No.11, Development Planning Unit, University College London.

Moser, Caroline and McIlwaine, Cathy (1999) 'A Guideline on Conceptual and Methodological Issues for Designing and Analysing the Results of Participatory Urban Appraisals (PUAs) in the Context of Violence', mimeo, LCSES, World Bank: Washington DC.

Moser, Caroline, Annika Tornqvist, and Bernice van Bronkhorst (1999) *Mainstreaming Gender and Development in the World Bank: Progress and Recommendations*, World Bank: Washington DC.

Neaz, Ahmad (1996) 'Converting Bangladesh's influential religious leaders', in *International Planned Parenthood Federation Challenges: Men's Needs and Responsibilities*, IPPF: London, 38–40.

Olavarría, José and Rodrigo Parrini (1999) 'Los padres adolescente/jóvenes: Hombres adolescentes y jóvenes frente al embarazo y nacimiento de un/a hijo/a. Antecedentes para la formulación y diseño de políticas públicas en Chile', unpublished ms, FLACSO: Santiago de Chile.

Overseas Development Administration (ODA) (1995) 'A Guide to Social Analysis for Projects in Developing Countries', HMSO: London.

Parpart, Jane (1995) 'Deconstructing the development "expert": gender, development and the "vulnerable groups"', in Marianne Marchand and Jane Parpart (eds), *Feminism/Postmodernism/Development*, Routledge: London, 221–43.

Parpart, Jane and Marianne Marchand (1995) 'Exploding the canon: an introduction and conclusion', in Marianne Marchand and Jane Parpart (eds), *Feminism/Postmodernism/Development*, Routledge: London, 1–22.

Pearson, Ruth (1999) 'Which Men? Why Now?', paper presented at ESRC Seminar 'Men, Masculinities and Gender Relations in Development: The Politics of the Personal', School of Development Studies, University of East Anglia, Norwich, 24–25 June.

Pearson, Ruth and Cecile Jackson (1998) 'Introduction: Interrogating development: feminism, gender and policy', in Cecile Jackson and Ruth Pearson (eds), *Feminist Visions of Development: Gender Analysis and Policy*, Routledge: London, 1–16.

Pietilä, Hilkka and Jeanne Vickers (1994) *Making Women Matter: The Role of the United Nations* (revised and expanded edition), Zed: London.

Pineda, Javier (2000) 'Partners in women-headed households: emerging masculinities', *European Journal of Development Research*, 12:2.

Piza-López, Eugenia (1994) 'GADU: a specialist gender unit in Oxfam', in Mandy MacDonald (ed.), *Gender Planning in Development Agencies: Meeting the Challenge*, Oxfam: Oxford, 58–66.

Porter, Fenella, Ines Smyth, and Caroline Sweetman (1999) 'Introduction', in Fenella Porter, Ines Smyth and Caroline Sweetman (eds), *Gender Works: Oxfam Experience in Policy and Practice*, Oxfam: Oxford, 1–13.

Quesada, Erick (1996) 'La masculinidad patriarcal y el anhelo de poder', in ILANUD, *Construcción de la Identidad Masculina*, Instituto Latinamericano de Naciones Unidas para la Prevención y Tratamiento del Delincuente: San José, 47–9.

Rathgeber, Eva (1995) 'Gender and development in action', in Marianne Marchand and Jane Parpart (eds), *Feminism/Postmodernism/Development*, Routledge: London, 204–20.

Rakodi, Carole (1991) 'Cities and people: towards a gender aware urban planning process?', *Public Administration and Development*, 11, 541–59.

Roche, Chris (1999) 'Middle-aged man seeks gender team', in Fenella Porter, Ines Smyth and Caroline Sweetman (eds), *Gender Works: Oxfam Experience in Policy and Practice*, Oxfam: Oxford, 203–10.

del Rosario, Virginia O. (1997) 'Mainstreaming gender concerns: aspects of compliance, resistance and negotiation', in Anne Marie Goetz (ed.), *Getting Institutions Right for Women in Development*, Zed: London, 77–89.

Royal Ministry of Foreign Affairs (1997) 'A Strategy for Women and Gender Equality in Development Cooperation', Royal Ministry of Foreign Affairs: Oslo.

Safilios-Rothschild, Constantina (1990) 'Socio-economic determinants of the outcomes of women's income-generation in developing countries', in Sharon Stichter and Jane Parpart (eds) *Women, Employment and the Family in the International Division of Labour*, (Macmillan: Basingstoke), 221–8.

Schifter, Jacobo (1998) *Lila's House: Male Prostitution in Latin America*, Hayworth: New York.

Scott, Catherine V. (1995) *Gender and Development: Rethinking Modernisation and Dependency Theory*, Lynne Rienner: Boulder, Colorado.

Sen, Gita and Caren Grown (1988) *Development, Crises and Alternative Visions*, Earthscan: London.

Shepard, Bonnie (1996) 'Masculinity and the male role in reproductive health', in *International Planned Parenthood Federation Challenges: Men's Needs and Responsibilities*, IPPF: London, 11–14.

Silberschmidt, Margrethe (1999) *'Women Forget that Men are the Masters': Gender Antagonism and Socio-economic Change in Kisii District, Kenya*, Nordiska Afrikainstitutet: Uppsala.

Smyke, Patricia (1991) *Women and Health*, Zed: London.

Smyth, Ines (1999) 'A rose by any other name: feminism in development NGOs', in Fenella Porter, Ines Smyth and Caroline Sweetman (eds), *Gender Works: Oxfam Experience in Policy and Practice*, Oxfam: Oxford, 132–41.

Staudt, Kathleen (1991) *Managing Development: State Society and International Contexts*, Sage: Newbury Park.

Sweetman, Caroline (1997) 'Editorial', in Caroline Sweetman (ed.), *Men and Masculinity*, Oxfam: Oxford, 2–6.

Sweetman, Caroline (1998) '"Sitting on a Rock": Integrating Men and Masculinities into Gender and Development', paper presented at ESRC Seminar 'Men, Masculinities and Gender Relations in Development', Development Project and Planning Centre, University of Bradford, 8–9 September.

Tadele, Feleke (1999) 'Men in the kitchen, women in the office? Working on gender issues in Ethiopia', in Fenella Porter, Ines Smyth and Caroline Sweetman (eds), *Gender Works: Oxfam Experience in Policy and Practice*, Oxfam: Oxford, 31–6.

Tomasevski, Katarina (1993) *Women and Human Rights*, Zed: London.

United Nations Development Programme (UNDP) (1995) *Human Development Report 1995*, Oxford University Press: New York.

United Nations Development Programme (UNDP) (1998) *Human Development Report 1998*, Oxford University Press: New York.

United Nations Development Fund for Women (UNIFEM)/Canadian International Development Agency — Southeast Asia Gender Equity Programme (CIDA-SEAGEP) (1998) *Women in a Global Economy: Challenge and Opportunity in the Current Asian Economic Crisis*, UNIFEM, East and Southeast Asia Regional Office/CIDA-SEAGEP: Singapore.

United Nations Educational, Scientific and Cultural Organisation (UNESCO) (1997) 'Male Roles and Masculinities in the Perspective of a Culture of Peace', report, Expert Group Meeting, Oslo, Norway, 24–28 September, UNESCO: Paris.

Vance, Irene (1985) 'More than bricks and mortar: women's participation in self-help housing in Managua, Nicaragua', in Caroline Moser and Linda Peake (eds), *Women, Human Settlements and Housing*, Tavistock: London, 139–65.

Versteylen, Tina (1994) 'Incorporating gender into Lomé IV projects and programmes', in Mandy MacDonald (ed.), *Gender Planning in Development Agencies: Meeting the Challenge*, Oxfam: Oxford, 177–84.

Viveros, Mara and William Cañon (1997) '"Pa" Bravo ... Yo soy Candela, Palo y Piedra, Los Quibdoseños', *ISIS International*, Ediciones de las Mujeres, FLACSO, Chile, 24, 125–38.

Viveros, Mara (1998) 'Decisiones reproductivas y dinámicas conyugales: el caso de la elección de la esterilización masculina', in Teresa Valdés and José Olavarría (eds), *Masculinidades y Equidad de Género en América Latina*, FLACSO/UNFPA: Santiago de Chile, 146–57.

Walker, Bridget (1994) 'Staff development and gender training in Oxfam', in Mandy MacDonald (ed.), *Gender Planning in Development Agencies: Meeting the Challenge*, Oxfam: Oxford, 148–57.

Wallace, Tina (1991) 'Case studies of ways of working with gender: introduction', in Tina Wallace with Candida March (eds) *Changing Perceptions: Writings on Gender and Development*, Oxfam: Oxford, 184–9.

Wallace, Tina with Candida March (eds) (1991) *Changing Perceptions: Writings on Gender and Development*, Oxfam: Oxford.

White, Sarah (1994) 'Making men an issue: gender planning for the other half', in Mandy MacDonald (ed.), *Gender Planning in Development Agencies: Meeting the Challenge*, Oxfam: Oxford, 98–110.

White, Sarah (1997) 'Men, masculinities and the politics of development', in Caroline Sweetman (ed.), *Men and Masculinity*, Oxfam: Oxford, 14–22.

Williams, Fiona (1998) 'Troubled masculinities in social policy discourses: fatherhood', in Jennie Popay, Jeff Hearn, and Jeanette Edwards (eds), *Men, Gender Divisions and Welfare*, Routledge: London, 63–97.

Williams, Suzanne (1999) 'Chronicle of a death foretold: the birth and death of Oxfam GB's gender and development unit', in Fenella Porter, Ines Smyth, and Caroline Sweetman (eds), *Gender Works: Oxfam Experience in Policy and Practice*, Oxfam: Oxford, 178–86.

Wood, Katherine and Rachel Jewkes (1997) 'Violence, rape and sexual coercion: everyday love in a South African Township', in Caroline Sweetman (ed.), *Men and Masculinity*, Oxfam: Oxford, 41–6.

Woodroffe, Jessica (1995) 'Pennies from Seven: Seven Ways the Group of Seven Summit can Help the Third World', Christian Aid: London.

World Bank (1990) 'Women in Development: A Progress Report on the World Bank Initiative', World Bank: Washington DC.

World Bank (1994) 'Enhancing Women's Participation in Economic Development', World Bank: Washington DC.

World Bank (1995) 'Advancing Gender Equality: From Concept to Action', World Bank: Washington DC.

Young, Kate (1993) *Planning Development With Women: Making a World of Difference*, Macmillan: Basingstoke.